UNIVERSITY OF ROCHESTER LIBRARIES

WITHDRAWN

Praise from the Experts

"The power of fixed effects models comes from their ability to control for observed and unobserved time-invariant variables that might confound an analysis. As knowledge of this feature of fixed effects models has spread, so has the interest in using these methods. One obstacle to further use has been the lack of accessible and consolidated information on fixed effects methods in diverse models such as linear regression, categorical and count regression, and event history models. A second obstacle to wider use has been insufficient knowledge of the software to implement these techniques.

"Paul Allison's *Fixed Effects Regression Methods for Longitudinal Data Using SAS®* goes a long way toward eliminating both barriers. This book is a clear, well-organized, and thoughtful guide to fixed effects models. There are separate chapters devoted to linear regression, categorical response variables, count data, and event history models. These models represent the most widely used ones in the social sciences. In a brief monograph, Allison is able to present the essentials of fixed effects for each model and the appropriate procedures in SAS that can implement them. Empirical examples and SAS code are included, making it easier for the reader to implement these methods.… In sum, Paul Allison has produced a terrific guide to fixed effects models and their estimation using SAS. I highly recommend it."

Kenneth A. Bollen
Immerwahr Distinguished Professor of Sociology
Director, Odum Institute for Research in Social Science
University of North Carolina at Chapel Hill

"*Fixed Effects Regression Methods for Longitudinal Data Using SAS* represents an excellent piece of work. It is clear, coherent, well-structured, useful, and has a sense of logical flow not always found in efforts of this sort. To say that I was impressed with this book would be an understatement.

"What I especially liked about the book was how Allison is able to fluidly mix clear and accurate explanations of statistical concerns and procedures with specific directions for how to go about these procedures in SAS. It merits observing that even researchers or students not thoroughly versed in the statistical underpinnings or mathematical complexities will be able to analyze and interpret their data using the directions provided. The author even provides sample outputs and takes the reader through a scholarly interpretation of results."

Frank Pajares
Professor of Educational Psychology
Division of Educational Studies
Emory University

SAS Press

Fixed Effects
Regression Methods
for Longitudinal Data
Using SAS

Paul D. Allison

The Power to Know.

The correct bibliographic citation for this manual is as follows: Allison, Paul D. 2005. *Fixed Effects Regression Methods for Longitudinal Data Using SAS®*. Cary, NC: SAS Institute Inc.

Fixed Effects Regression Methods for Longitudinal Data Using SAS®

Copyright © 2005, SAS Institute Inc., Cary, NC, USA

ISBN 1-59047-568-2

All rights reserved. Produced in the United States of America.

For a hard-copy book: No part of this publication may be reproduced, stored in a retrieval system, or transmitted, in any form or by any means, electronic, mechanical, photocopying, or otherwise, without the prior written permission of the publisher, SAS Institute Inc.

For a Web download or e-book: Your use of this publication shall be governed by the terms established by the vendor at the time you acquire this publication.

U.S. Government Restricted Rights Notice: Use, duplication, or disclosure of this software and related documentation by the U.S. government is subject to the Agreement with SAS Institute and the restrictions set forth in FAR 52.227-19, Commercial Computer Software-Restricted Rights (June 1987).

SAS Institute Inc., SAS Campus Drive, Cary, North Carolina 27513.

1st printing, March 2005

SAS Publishing provides a complete selection of books and electronic products to help customers use SAS software to its fullest potential. For more information about our e-books, e-learning products, CDs, and hard-copy books, visit the SAS Publishing Web site at **support.sas.com/pubs** or call 1-800-727-3228.

SAS® and all other SAS Institute Inc. product or service names are registered trademarks or trademarks of SAS Institute Inc. in the USA and other countries. ® indicates USA registration.

Other brand and product names are registered trademarks or trademarks of their respective companies.

Contents

Acknowledgments

For their detailed comments and suggestions, I would like to thank Andrew Karp, Guang Guo, Mike Patteta and David Schlotzhauer. For permission to use their data in the examples, I am indebted to Nicholas Christakis, Paula England, Sharon Harlan, Anne Keane, and Peter Tice. As usual, my editor, Judy Whatley, deserves a huge amount of credit for persistently but gently prodding me to finish this book.

Introduction to Fixed Effects Methods

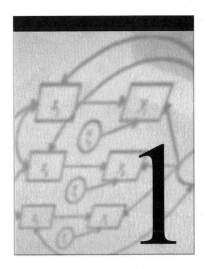

1.1 The Promise of Fixed Effects for Nonexperimental Research

Every empirical researcher knows that randomized experiments have major advantages over observational studies in making causal inferences. Randomization of subjects to different treatment conditions ensures that the treatment groups, on average, are identical with respect to all possible characteristics of the subjects, regardless of whether those characteristics can be measured or not. If the subjects are people, for example, the treatment groups produced by randomization will be approximately equal with respect to such easily measured variables as race, sex, and age, and also approximately equal for more problematic variables like intelligence, aggressiveness, and creativity.

In nonexperimental studies, researchers often try to approximate a randomized experiment by statistically controlling for other variables using methods such as linear regression, logistic regression, or propensity scores. While statistical control can certainly be a useful tactic, it has two major limitations. First, no matter how many variables you control for, someone can always criticize your study by suggesting that you left out some crucial variable. (Such critiques are more compelling when that crucial variable is named). As is well known, the omission of a key covariate can lead to severe bias in estimating the effects of the variables that are included. Second, to statistically control for a variable, you have to measure it and explicitly include it in some kind of model. The problem is that some variables are notoriously difficult to measure. If the measurement is imperfect (and it usually is), this can also lead to biased estimates. So in practice, causal inference via statistical adjustment usually runs a poor second to the randomized experiment.

It turns out, however, that with certain kinds of nonexperimental data we can get much closer to the virtues of a randomized experiment. Specifically, by using the fixed effects methods discussed in this book, it is possible to control for all possible characteristics of the individuals in the study—even without measuring them—so long as those characteristics do not change over time. I realize that this is a powerful claim, and it is one that I will take pains to justify as we go along. What is also remarkable is that fixed effects methods have been lying under our noses for many years. If the dependent variable is quantitative, then fixed effects methods can be easily implemented using ordinary least squares linear regression. When the dependent variable is categorical, somewhat more sophisticated methods are necessary, but even then the fixed effects approach is a lot easier than many alternative methods.

There are two key data requirements for the application of a fixed effects method. First, each individual in the sample must have two or more measurements on the same dependent variable. Second, for at least some of the individuals in the sample, the values of the independent variable(s) of interest must be different on at least two of the measurement occasions.

1.2 The Paired-Comparisons *t*-Test as a Fixed Effects Method

Perhaps the simplest design that meets these two requirements is a before-after study. Suppose, for example, that 100 people volunteer to participate in a weight loss program. They all get weighed when they enter the study, producing the variable W_1. All 100 people are then given a new medication believed to facilitate weight loss. After two months on this medication, they are weighed again, producing the variable W_2. So we have measurements of weight on two occasions for each participant. The participants are off the medication for the first measurement and are on the medication for the second.

How should such data be analyzed? Before answering that question, let's first concede that this is not an ideal study design, most importantly because there is no control group of people who don't receive the medication at either time. Nevertheless, the application of fixed effects methods has all the virtues that I claimed above. The objective here is to test the null hypothesis that mean weight at time 1 is the same as mean weight at time 2, against the alternative that mean weight is lower at time 2. In this case, an easily applied fixed effects method is one that is taught in most introductory statistics courses under the name of paired-comparisons *t*-test or paired-differences *t*-test. The steps are:

1. Form $D = W_2 - W_1$.

2. Calculate $\overline{D}$, the mean of D.

3. Test whether $\overline{D}$ is significantly less than 0.

The third step is accomplished by dividing $\overline{D}$ by its estimated standard error $s / \sqrt{n}$, where s is the sample standard deviation of D, and n is the sample size. The resulting test statistic has a *t* distribution with $n - 1$ degrees of freedom under the null hypothesis (assuming that D is normally distributed).

If $\overline{D}$ is significantly less than 0, what can we conclude? Well, we can't be sure that the medication caused the weight loss, because it's possible that something else happened to these people between time 1 and time 2. However, we *can* be sure that the difference in average weight between the two time points is not explainable by stable characteristics of the people in the study. In other words, we can be quite confident that the weight loss was *not* produced by changes in race, gender, parental wealth, or intelligence.

While this conclusion may seem obvious, it's helpful to consider a mathematical formulation as a way of introducing some of the ideas that underlie the more complicated models considered later. Let

$$W_{i1} = \mu + \alpha_i + \varepsilon_{i1}$$
$$W_{i2} = \mu + \delta + \alpha_i + \varepsilon_{i2}$$

where W_{i1} is the weight of person i at time 1, and similarly W_{i2} is the weight at time 2. In this model, μ is the baseline average weight, and δ denotes the change in the average from time 1 to time 2. The disturbance terms ε_{i1} and ε_{i2} represent random variation that is specific to a particular individual at a particular point in time. As in other linear models, one might assume that ε_{i1} and ε_{i2} each have an expected value of 0. The term α_i represents all the person-specific variation that is *stable* over time. Thus α_i can be thought to include the effects of such variables as race, gender, parental wealth, and intelligence.

When we form the difference score, we get

$$D_i = \delta + \left(\varepsilon_{i2} - \varepsilon_{i1}\right)$$

which shows that both the baseline mean μ and the stable individual variation α_i disappear when we compute difference scores. Therefore, the stable individual differences can have no effect on our conclusions, even if α_i is correlated with ε_{i1} or ε_{i2}.

The essence of a fixed effects method is captured by saying that each individual serves as his or her own control. That is accomplished by making comparisons *within* individuals (hence the need for at least two measurements), and then averaging those differences across all the individuals in the sample. How this is accomplished depends greatly on the characteristics of the data and the design of the study.

1.3 Costs and Benefits of Fixed Effects Methods

As already noted, the major attraction of fixed effects methods in nonexperimental research is the ability to control for all stable characteristics of the individuals in the study, thereby eliminating potentially large sources of bias. Within-subject comparisons have also been popular in certain kinds of designed experiments known as changeover or crossover designs (Senn 1993). In these designs, subjects receive different treatments at different times, and a response variable is measured for each treatment. Ideally, the order in which the treatments are received is randomized. The objective of the crossover design is not primarily to reduce bias, but to reduce sampling variability and hence produce more powerful tests of hypotheses.

The rationale is that by differencing out the individual variability across subjects, one can eliminate much of the error variance that is present with conventional experimental designs in which each subject receives only one treatment.

By contrast, when fixed effects methods are applied to nonexperimental data, there is often an *increase* in sampling variability relative to alternative methods of analysis. The reason is that in the typical observational study, the independent variables of interest vary both within and between subjects. Suppose, for example, that one of the independent variables is personal income, measured annually for five successive years. While there might be considerable within-person variation in income over time, the bulk of the variation is likely to be between persons.

Fixed effects methods completely ignore the between-person variation and focus only on the within-person variation. Unfortunately, discarding the between-person variation can yield standard errors that are considerably higher than those produced by methods that utilize both within- and between-person variation. So why do it? The answer is that the between-person variation is very likely to be contaminated by unmeasured personal characteristics that are correlated with income. By restricting ourselves to the within-person variation, we eliminate that contamination and are much more likely to get unbiased estimates.

So what we're dealing with is a trade-off between bias and sampling variability. For nonexperimental data, fixed effects methods tend to reduce bias at the expense of greater sampling variability. Given the many reasons for expecting bias in observational studies, I think this is usually an attractive bargain. Nevertheless, one crucial limitation to fixed effects methods arises when the ratio of within- to between-person variance declines to 0: *fixed effects methods cannot estimate coefficients for variables that have no within-subject variation.* Hence, a fixed effects method will not give you coefficients for race, sex, or region of birth. Among adults, it won't be very helpful in estimating effects of height or years of schooling (although there may be a little within-person variation on the latter). Keep in mind, however, that all these stable variables are *controlled* in a fixed effects regression, even if there are no measurements of them. In fact, the control is likely to be much more effective than in conventional regression. And as we'll see later, you *can* include interactions between stable variables such as sex and variables that vary over time. But for most observational studies, fixed effects methods are primarily useful for investigating the effects of variables that vary within subject.

For experimental data, the situation with respect to bias and sampling variability is exactly reversed. Bias is eliminated by giving the same set of treatments to all subjects and by randomizing the order in which the treatments are presented. The result is approximately zero correlation between treatment and stable characteristics of the subjects, which means that there is no need for fixed effects to reduce bias. On the other hand, by design, all the variation on the independent variables (the treatments) is within subjects. So no information is lost by restricting attention to the within-subject variation. Indeed, standard errors can be greatly reduced by fixed effects methods because the error term has smaller variance.

1.4 Why Are These Methods Called "Fixed Effects"?

The name "fixed effects" is a source of considerable confusion. As we shall see, the basic idea is very simple. Consider the linear model

$$Y_{ij} = \beta_0 + \beta_1 x_{ij} + \alpha_i + \varepsilon_{ij}$$

where the i subscript refers to different persons and j refers to different measurements within persons—i.e., the same variable measured at different points in time. In conventional linear model terminology, $\beta_1 x_{ij}$ is described as a fixed effect because the x_{ij} terms are all measured values and β_1 is a fixed parameter. On the other hand, ε_{ij} is regarded as a random variable with a probability distribution, and we make certain assumptions about this distribution. For example, we might assume that ε_{ij} has a normal distribution with mean 0 and variance σ^2. So the typical linear model has both fixed components and random components.

What about the term α_i, which we use to represent all stable characteristics of persons? Here we have an important choice between treating α_i as either fixed or random. Some methods, such as the so-called mixed models estimated by PROC MIXED, treat α_i as a random variable with a specified probability distribution (usually normal, homoscedastic, and independent of all measured variables). In the econometric literature, these are called random effects models. In fixed effects models, however, the α_i term is treated as a set of fixed parameters, which may either be estimated directly or conditioned out of the estimation process. Hence the name, "fixed effects."

Which is better, fixed effects or random effects? That depends on your objectives. In the preceding section, I already described the advantages and disadvantages of fixed effects methods. The advantages and disadvantages of random effects methods are the mirror image. Random effects methods do *not* control for unmeasured, stable characteristics of the individuals. That's because the α_i terms are virtually always assumed to be uncorrelated with the measured variables that are included in the model. On the other hand, with random effects you can estimate the effects of stable covariates such as race and gender. And because they use variation both within and between individuals, random effects methods typically have less sampling variability than fixed effects methods. Although the primary focus of this book is on fixed effects methods, I will often contrast those methods with alternative random effects approaches.

In my view, then, the decision to treat the between-person variation as fixed or random should depend largely on

- whether it's important to control for unmeasured characteristics of individuals
- whether it's important to estimate the effects of stable covariates
- whether one can tolerate the substantial loss of information that comes from discarding the between-individual variation

In the literature on ANOVA and experimental design, however, the decision between fixed and random effects is often described in quite different terms. Consider the following characterization:

> Common practice is to regard the treatment effects as fixed if those treatment
> levels used are the only ones about which inferences are sought . . . . If
> inferences are sought about a broader collection of treatment effects than
> those used in the experiment, or if the treatment levels are not selected
> purposefully . . . , it is common practice to regard the treatment effects as
> random (LaMotte 1983, pp. 138–139).

According to this view, it would nearly always make more sense to treat the between-person variation represented by α_i as random, because then one can make inferences to broader populations than the sample in hand. But for the kinds of applications considered in this book, I believe that argument is mistaken, for two reasons. First, the purpose of including α_i in the equation is usually *not* because we want to estimate or test hypotheses about the between-person effects. Instead, the goal is to estimate the coefficients of *other* variables while *controlling* for unmeasured covariates and adjusting for lack of independence among the multiple observations for each person. For these purposes, it's irrelevant whether inferences about α_i can or cannot be generalized to larger populations. Second, fixed effects models are generally much less restrictive than random effects models, and thus these models are more likely to represent the data in a realistic way. In fact, for linear models it has been shown that random effects estimators are a special case of fixed effects estimators (Mundlak 1978).

1.5 Fixed Effects Methods in SAS/STAT

Different kinds of dependent variables require different kinds of fixed effects methods. SAS has a variety of procedures that can be used to implement fixed effects methods, although the original programmers may not have had such applications in mind. For linear models, PROC GLM is probably the most convenient procedure for performing a fixed effects analysis, although PROC REG and PROC MIXED can also be used with a little effort. For fixed effects logistic regression, PROC LOGISTIC is the most convenient procedure, but PROC GENMOD can be used in applications where there are only two observations per individual. For fixed effects Poisson regression, PROC GENMOD appears to be the only choice. For fixed effects survival analysis, PROC PHREG is the procedure of choice, although PROC LOGISTIC can be used in some circumstances. Finally, PROC CALIS can be useful for fitting fixed effects linear models with lagged endogenous variables.

1.6 What You Need to Know

To understand this book, how much you should already know depends on how far you want to go. To read chapter 2 on linear models, you need to be familiar with multiple linear regression. That means that you should know something about the assumptions of the linear regression model and about estimation of the model via ordinary least squares. Ideally, you should have a substantial amount of practical experience using multiple regression on real data and should feel comfortable interpreting the output from a regression analysis. As part of this knowledge, you must certainly know the basic principles of statistical inference: standard errors, confidence intervals, hypothesis tests, p-values, bias, efficiency, and so on.

To read chapter 3, you should have, in addition to the requirements for chapter 2, a knowledge of logistic regression at about the level of the first three chapters of my 1999 book *Logistic Regression Using the SAS System: Theory and Application*. That is, you should understand the basic model for binary logistic regression, how to estimate that model via maximum likelihood, and how to interpret the results in terms of odds ratios. Some familiarity with PROC LOGISTIC is helpful, but not essential.

For chapter 4 on fixed effects Poisson regression, you should have a basic familiarity with the Poisson regression model, discussed in chapter 9 of *Logistic Regression Using the SAS System: Theory and Application.* I'll use PROC GENMOD to estimate the model, so previous experience with this procedure will be helpful.

For chapter 5 on survival analysis, some basic knowledge of the Cox proportional hazards model and partial likelihood estimation is essential. These methods are described in my 1995 book *Survival Analysis Using SAS: A Practical Guide,* along with instruction on how to use the PHREG procedure.

Finally, to read chapter 6 you should have some knowledge of linear structural equation models (SEMs) that include both observed and latent variables. A good introduction to this topic for SAS users is *A Step-by-Step Approach to Using the SAS System for Factor Analysis and Structural Equation Modeling* (Hatcher 1994).

I have tried to keep the mathematics to a minimal level throughout the book. In particular, there is no calculus and little use of matrix notation. Nevertheless, to simplify the presentation of regression models, I frequently use the vector notation $\beta x = \beta_0 + \beta_1 x_1 + ... + \beta_k x_k$. While it would be helpful to have some knowledge of maximum likelihood estimation, it's hardly essential. With regard to SAS, the more experience you have with SAS/STAT and the SAS DATA step, the easier it will be to follow the presentation of SAS programs. On the other hand, most of the programs presented in this book are fairly simple and short, so don't be intimidated if you're just beginning to learn SAS.

1.7 Computing

All the computer input and output displayed in this book was produced by and for SAS 9.1 for Windows. Occasionally I point out differences between the syntax of SAS 9.1 and earlier releases. I use the following convention for presenting SAS programs: All words that are part of the SAS language are shown in upper case. All user-specified variable names and data set names are in lower case. In the main text itself, both SAS keywords and user-specified variables are in upper case.

The output displays were produced with the SAS Output Delivery System. To avoid unnecessary distraction, I do not include the ODS statements in the programs shown in the book. However, the reader who would like to duplicate those displays can do so with the following code before and after the procedure statements:

```
OPTIONS LS=75 PS=3000 NODATE NOCENTER NONUMBER;
ODS LISTING CLOSE;
ODS RTF FILE='c:\book.rtf' STYLE=JOURNAL BODYTITLE;

---PROC STATEMENTS HERE---

ODS RTF CLOSE;
ODS LISTING;
```

All the examples were run on a Dell Optiplex GX270 desktop computer running Windows XP at 3 gigahertz with 1 gibabyte of physical memory.

Fixed Effects Methods for Linear Regression

2.1 Introduction

In chapter 1, I showed how the conventional paired-comparisons t-test could be interpreted as a fixed effects method that controlled for all stable characteristics of the individual. The model discussed there was actually a special case of a more general linear model for quantitative response variables. That model is the subject of this chapter.

First some notation. Let y_{it} be the value of the response variable for individual i on occasion t. To keep things concrete, I'll refer to the individuals as persons and the occasions as different times at which the person is measured. However, in some applications i could index groups and t could index different individuals within those groups.

We also have some predictor variables: z_i is a column vector of variables that describe persons but do not vary over time; x_{it} is a column vector of variables that vary both over individuals and over time for each individual. (If you're not comfortable with vectors, you can read these as single variables). The basic model that we will use is

$$y_{it} = \mu_t + \beta x_{it} + \gamma z_i + \alpha_i + \varepsilon_{it} \qquad i = 1,\dots, n; \, t = 1,\dots, T \qquad (2.1)$$

In this equation μ_t is an intercept that is allowed to vary with time, β and γ are row vectors of coefficients, and ε_{it} is a random disturbance term. As in chapter 1, α_i represents all differences between persons that are stable over time and not otherwise accounted for by γz_i. In a fixed effects model, we regard these as fixed parameters, one per person. That implies that x_{it} may be correlated with α_i.

As in the conventional linear model, we assume that ε_{it} has a mean of 0, that it has constant variance, and that $cov(\varepsilon_{it}, \varepsilon_{jt}) = 0$ for $i \neq j$. Unlike conventional linear regression, we do not require that ε_{it} be uncorrelated with z_i or α_i. On the other hand, the assumptions about the relationship between ε_{it} and x_{it} are somewhat stronger than usual. Specifically, for the methods used in this chapter, we assume that x_{it} is *strictly exogenous*, which means that x_{it} at any time t is statistically independent of the random disturbances at all points in time, not just at time t. The most important aspect of this assumption is that x_{it} cannot depend on y at earlier points in time. In chapter 6, however, we shall relax this assumption to allow for reciprocal relationships between the two variables.

Under these assumptions, equation (2.1) can be optimally estimated by ordinary least squares (OLS). However, depending in part on the structure of the data, there are a variety of ways to implement OLS for the fixed effects model and a number of special considerations that need to be addressed. Let's first see how to do it in the relatively simple situation in which each individual has exactly two measurements on both the response variable and the time-varying predictor variables.

2.2 Estimation with Two Observations Per Person

When there are exactly two observations per person ($t = 1, 2$), estimation of the fixed effects model can be easily accomplished by OLS regression using difference scores for all the time-varying variables. The equations for the two time points are

$$\begin{aligned} y_{i1} &= \mu_1 + \beta x_{i1} + \gamma z_i + \alpha_i + \varepsilon_{i1} \\ y_{i2} &= \mu_2 + \beta x_{i2} + \gamma z_i + \alpha_i + \varepsilon_{i2} \end{aligned} \qquad (2.2)$$

Subtracting the first equation from the second, we get

$$y_{i2} - y_{i1} = (\mu_2 - \mu_1) + \beta(x_{i2} - x_{i1}) + (\varepsilon_{i2} - \varepsilon_{i1}) \qquad (2.3)$$

Notice that both γz_i and α_i have been "differenced out" of the equation. Consequently, we cannot estimate γ, the coefficients for the time-invariant predictors. Nevertheless, this method completely controls for the effects of these variables. Furthermore, if ε_{i1} and ε_{i2} both satisfy the assumptions of the standard linear model, then their difference will also satisfy those assumptions (even if ε_{i1} and ε_{i2} are correlated). So OLS applied to the difference scores should give unbiased and efficient estimates of β, the coefficients for the time-varying predictors.

Let's try this on some real data. The sample consists of 581 children who were interviewed in 1990, 1992, and 1994 as part of the National Longitudinal Survey of Youth (Center for Human Resource Research 2002). We'll look at three variables that were measured in each of the three interviews:

ANTI   antisocial behavior, measured with a scale ranging from 0 to 6

SELF   self-esteem, measured with a scale ranging from 6 to 24

POV   poverty status of family, coded 1 for in poverty, otherwise 0

In this section, we will use only the data from 1990 and 1994. Our goal is to estimate a regression model of the form:

$$\text{ANTI}(t) = \mu(t) + \beta_1\text{SELF}(t) + \beta_2\text{POV}(t) + \varepsilon(t)$$

for $t = 1, 2$. That is, we shall assume that poverty and self-esteem at time t affect antisocial behavior at the same time. I recognize that there may be uncertainties about causal ordering for these variables, but such difficulties will be ignored in this chapter. A related issue is whether the independent variables should be lagged, but with only two time points, it's impossible to estimate a model with both lags and fixed effects. Another implicit assumption is that the regression coefficients are the same at each time point, but that assumption can be tested or relaxed, as we'll see later.

As a point of departure, I begin by estimating the regression equation for each year separately using PROC REG. The SAS data set MY.NLSY has one observation per person, with separate variables for the measurements in the different years. The following SAS code is used for estimating the model:

```
PROC REG DATA=my.nlsy;
   MODEL anti90=self90 pov90;
   MODEL anti94=self94 pov94;
RUN;
```

Please note that this and all other data sets used in this book are available for download at support.sas.com/companionsites.

Selected portions of the output are displayed in Output 2.1. We see that both of the independent variables are statistically significant at beyond the .05 level in both years. As one might expect, higher self esteem is associated with lower levels of antisocial behavior, whereas poverty is associated with higher levels of antisocial behavior. The effect of SELF is slightly larger in 1994 than in 1990, while the reverse is true for POV.

Output 2.1 Regressions of ANTI on POV and SELF in 1990 and 1994

Dependent Variable: anti90 child antisocial behavior in 1990

Variable	DF	Parameter Estimate	Standard Error	t Value	Pr > |t|
Intercept	1	2.37482	0.38447	6.18	<.0001
self90	1	-0.05014	0.01870	-2.68	0.0075
pov90	1	0.59473	0.12629	4.71	<.0001

Dependent Variable: anti94 child antisocial behavior in 1994

Variable	DF	Parameter Estimate	Standard Error	t Value	Pr > |t|
Intercept	1	2.88797	0.44688	6.46	<.0001
self94	1	-0.06388	0.02113	-3.02	0.0026
pov94	1	0.54712	0.14765	3.71	0.0002

The problem with these regressions is that they do not control for any time-invariant variables. Rather than putting such variables into the model, we'll proceed directly to the difference equation, which controls for *all* time-invariant variables. To do this, we first need a DATA step to create the difference scores:

```
DATA diff;
   SET my.nlsy;
   antidiff=anti94-anti90;
   povdiff=pov94-pov90;
   selfdiff=self94-self90;
PROC REG DATA=diff;
   MODEL antidiff=selfdiff povdiff;
RUN;
```

Results are shown in Output 2.2. The coefficient for SELFDIFF is about midway between the two coefficients for SELF in Output 2.1, but the coefficient for POVDIFF is markedly lower than the two coefficients in Output 2.1 and is far from statistically significant. It thus appears that although there might be an association between poverty status and antisocial behavior, that association is largely cross-sectional and is perhaps explainable by their mutual dependence on other variables. But *changes* in poverty status do not seem to be associated with *changes* in antisocial behavior.

Output 2.2 Regression with Difference Scores

Dependent Variable: antidiff

Variable	DF	Parameter Estimate	Standard Error	t Value	Pr > |t|
Intercept	1	0.20923	0.06305	3.32	0.0010
selfdiff	1	-0.05615	0.01531	-3.67	0.0003
povdiff	1	-0.03631	0.12827	-0.28	0.7772

One concern is that there might be too few changes in poverty status to reliably estimate the effect of this variable. Output 2.3 shows that although the majority of children did not change in status, about 24% did change in one direction or another. This change should be sufficient to get a reliable estimate. In fact, the standard error for the poverty coefficient in the difference equation is about the same as the smaller of the two standard errors for the cross-sectional coefficients in Output 2.1.

Output 2.3 Cross-Tabulation of Poverty Status in 1990 and 1994

	pov90	pov94		
Frequency		0	1	Total
	0	321	65	386
	1	73	122	195
Total		394	187	581

Regression with difference scores is not the only way to produce OLS estimates of the fixed effects model for these data. The following alternative method is computationally cumbersome, but instructive. The first step is to reorganize the data so that, instead of one observation per person, there is one observation per person-year. The same variable name is used for the measurements of each conceptual variable in the two years. The new data set also contains an ID variable that has the same value for both years for the same person, and a TIME variable with a value of 0 for 1990 and 1 for 1994. Here is the SAS code to produce this new data set:

```
DATA persyr2;
    SET my.nlsy;
    id=_N_;
    time=0;
    anti=anti90;
    self=self90;
    pov=pov90;
    OUTPUT;
    time=1;
    anti=anti94;
    self=self94;
    pov=pov94;
    OUTPUT;
RUN;
```

The new data set has 1162 observations, two for each of the 581 children. Equation (2.1) is now estimated in its original form

$$y_{it} = \mu_t + \beta x_{it} + \alpha_i + \varepsilon_{it}$$

except that γz_i is removed because it is perfectly collinear with α_i. To allow for different intercepts in the two years, the regression includes the TIME variable. To estimate the α_i terms, the regression model includes 580 dummy variables, one for each child except the last. This would be awkward in PROC REG because all the dummies would have to be created in a DATA step. It's easy in PROC GLM, however, because the CLASS statement can create the dummies automatically:

```
PROC GLM DATA=persyr2;
   CLASS id;
   MODEL anti=self pov time id / SOLUTION;
RUN;
```

The SOLUTION option tells GLM to print out the coefficient estimates and their associated statistics. (This is unnecessary when there are no CLASS variables). Selected results are shown in Output 2.4. Only the first 10 coefficients for the dummy variables are shown.

The most important fact about this output is that the coefficients for SELF and POV (along with their standard errors, *t*-statistics, and *p*-values) are identical to those in Output 2.2, which was based on the difference equation. Furthermore, the coefficient for TIME is identical to the intercept in Output 2.2. So it seems that we get equivalent results using these two computational methods. But the dummy variable method is much slower than the difference score method because it requires the inversion of a very large matrix. On my PC, PROC REG took .01 seconds to estimate the difference-score model, whereas PROC GLM took 3.3 seconds to estimate the dummy variable model.

Output 2.4 PROC GLM Results for Person-Year Data Set

Parameter		Estimate	Standard Error	t Value	Pr > |t|
Intercept		1.508435913	0.81214706	1.86	0.0638
self		-0.056148639	0.01530506	-3.67	0.0003
pov		-0.036308618	0.12827438	-0.28	0.7772
time		0.209233732	0.06305436	3.32	0.0010
id	1	0.658525908	1.06750664	0.62	0.5376
id	2	-0.377782710	1.06740470	-0.35	0.7235
id	3	4.650291609	1.06769622	4.36	<.0001

continued

Output 2.4 *(continued)*

Parameter		Estimate	Standard Error	t Value	Pr > |t|
id	4	1.122217290	1.06740470	1.05	0.2935
id	5	0.178365929	1.06804248	0.17	0.8674
id	6	0.594142970	1.06716799	0.56	0.5779
id	7	2.925697051	1.06689988	2.74	0.0063
id	8	1.869548412	1.06724956	1.75	0.0803
id	9	0.037994330	1.06685908	0.04	0.9716
id	10	4.313399772	1.06781851	4.04	<.0001

Using the same person-year data configuration, it's possible to greatly reduce the computation time by not explicitly estimating the dummy variable coefficients. I'll explain this method in more detail in section 2.4, but let's first look at how it is implemented. In PROC GLM, we take the variable ID out of the MODEL and CLASS statements, and we put it in an ABSORB statement instead. Here is the new program:

```
PROC GLM DATA=persyr2;
    ABSORB id;
    MODEL anti=self pov time;
RUN;
```

This program took about the same computing time as using PROC REG with the difference scores. It's apparent that the results in Output 2.5 are identical to those found in Outputs 2.4 and 2.2. As we'll see in section 2.4, this last method for OLS estimation of the fixed effects model is generally preferred when there are more than two observations per person.

Output 2.5 GLM Results Using the ABSORB Statement

Parameter	Estimate	Standard Error	t Value	Pr > |t|
self	-.0561486395	0.01530506	-3.67	0.0003
pov	-.0363086183	0.12827438	-0.28	0.7772
time	0.2092337322	0.06305436	3.32	0.0010

2.3 Extending the Model

The model of equation (2.2) is somewhat restrictive because it assumes that the regression slopes are invariant across time. This assumption can be tested and relaxed. Consider the model

$$y_{i1} = \mu_1 + \beta_1 x_{i1} + \gamma z_i + \alpha_i + \varepsilon_{i1}$$
$$y_{i2} = \mu_2 + \beta_2 x_{i2} + \gamma z_i + \alpha_i + \varepsilon_{i2}$$

(2.4)

which is identical to equation (2.2) except that the β coefficient is allowed to differ for times 1 and 2. The difference score equation then becomes

$$y_{i2} - y_{i1} = (\mu_2 - \mu_1) + \beta_2 x_{i2} - \beta_1 x_{i1} + (\varepsilon_{i2} - \varepsilon_{i1})$$

which, with a little algebra, can also be written as

$$y_{i2} - y_{i1} = (\mu_2 - \mu_1) + \beta_2 (x_{i2} - x_{i1}) + (\beta_2 - \beta_1) x_{i1} + (\varepsilon_{i2} - \varepsilon_{i1})$$

This equation says that both $(x_2 - x_1)$ and x_1 should appear as independent variables in the difference equation. If the coefficient for x_1 is significantly different from 0, that's evidence that β_1 and β_2 are not equal.

Let's try it for the NLSY data. Here is the program:

```
PROC REG DATA=diff;
   MODEL antidiff=selfdiff povdiff self90 pov90;
RUN;
```

Results in Output 2.6 provide no evidence that the effects of poverty and self-esteem on antisocial behavior are different in 1990 and 1994. Both coefficients for the time 1 variables are far from statistically significant.

Output 2.6 Difference Regression with Time 1 Variables

Variable	DF	Parameter Estimate	Standard Error	t Value	Pr > |t|
Intercept	1	0.64837	0.52113	1.24	0.2139
selfdiff	1	-0.06685	0.01960	-3.41	0.0007
povdiff	1	-0.01410	0.15110	-0.09	0.9257
self90	1	-0.02226	0.02511	-0.89	0.3757
pov90	1	0.04126	0.15626	0.26	0.7919

Another way to extend the model is to allow the coefficients for the time-invariant variables to change with time, as in

$$y_{i1} = \mu_1 + \beta x_{i1} + \gamma_1 z_i + \alpha_i + \varepsilon_{i1}$$
$$y_{i2} = \mu_2 + \beta x_{i2} + \gamma_2 z_i + \alpha_i + \varepsilon_{i2}$$

Here, the γ coefficient is allowed to differ at the two time points, leading to the difference equation

$$y_{i2} - y_{i1} = (\mu_2 - \mu_1) + \beta_2 (x_{i2} - x_{i1}) + (\gamma_2 - \gamma_1) z_i + (\varepsilon_{i2} - \varepsilon_{i1})$$

In this case z does not drop out of the equation and must be included in the regression model. This result teaches us that fixed effects regression only controls for those time-invariant variables whose effects on the dependent variable are also time invariant. If a variable does not have time-invariant effects, it must be explicitly included in the model.

The NLSY data set has several time-invariant variables that are worth examining as possible predictors:

BLACK   1 if child is black, otherwise 0

HISPANIC   1 if child is Hispanic, otherwise 0

CHILDAGE   child's age in 1990

MARRIED   1 if mother was currently married in 1990, otherwise 0

GENDER   1 if female, 0 if male

MOMAGE   mother's age at birth of child

MOMWORK   1 if mother was employed in 1990, otherwise 0

These variables are now included in the difference score regression:

```
PROC REG DATA=diff;
   MODEL antidiff=selfdiff povdiff black hispanic childage
         married gender momage momwork;
RUN;
```

Results in Output 2.7 show that only one of the time-invariant variables, CHILDAGE, has a coefficient that even approaches statistical significance. And the inclusion of the time-invariant variables has very little impact on the coefficient estimates for SELFDIFF and POVDIFF. We conclude that there is some evidence that the effect of CHILDAGE is different in 1990 and 1994, but there is little or no evidence for a change over time in the effects of the other time-invariant variables.

Output 2.7 Difference Regression with Time Invariant Variables

Variable	DF	Parameter Estimate	Standard Error	t Value	Pr > |t|
Intercept	1	-0.82002	1.27227	-0.64	0.5195
selfdiff	1	-0.05275	0.01554	-3.39	0.0007
povdiff	1	-0.02670	0.12996	-0.21	0.8373
black	1	-0.06179	0.14583	-0.42	0.6720
hispanic	1	0.10518	0.16257	0.65	0.5179
childage	1	0.21953	0.10735	2.05	0.0413
married	1	-0.17487	0.14921	-1.17	0.2417
gender	1	0.11065	0.12584	0.88	0.3796
momage	1	-0.04415	0.02972	-1.49	0.1379
momwork	1	-0.12445	0.13270	-0.94	0.3487

Results using the difference score method can also be replicated on the person-year data set, using PROC GLM with the ABSORB statement. To test for changes in the coefficients for SELF and POV, we include interactions between these variables and TIME:

```
PROC GLM DATA=persyr2;
   ABSORB id;
   MODEL anti=self pov time self*time pov*time;
RUN;
```

Results in Output 2.8 are equivalent to those in Output 2.6.

Output 2.8 GLM with Interactions between TIME and Time-Varying Covariates

Parameter	Estimate	Standard Error	t Value	Pr > |t|
self	-.0445833075	0.02002789	-2.23	0.0264
pov	-.0553562291	0.14951835	-0.37	0.7113
time	0.6483709742	0.52113018	1.24	0.2139
self*time	-.0222626258	0.02511098	-0.89	0.3757
pov*time	0.0412572182	0.15625947	0.26	0.7919

To replicate the results in Output 2.7, we can use PROC GLM with interactions between TIME and the time-invariant predictors:

```
PROC GLM DATA=persyr2;
   ABSORB id;
   MODEL anti=self pov time black*time hispanic*time
         childage*time married*time gender*time
         momage*time momwork*time;
RUN;
```

Results in Output 2.9 are, in fact, equivalent to those in Output 2.7. Note that although the model includes interactions between TIME and the time-invariant predictors, it does not include the "main effects" of those covariates. While this may seem contrary to conventional practice, it is not a problem for this kind of analysis. In fact, if you tried to include the main effects, GLM would report coefficients of 0 with 0 degrees of freedom. That's because the time-invariant variables are perfectly collinear with the α_i parameters that have been "conditioned" out of the regression equation.

Output 2.9 GLM with Interactions between TIME and Time-Invariant Covariates

Parameter	Estimate	Standard Error	t Value	Pr > |t|
self	-.0527540181	0.01554026	-3.39	0.0007
pov	-.0267038294	0.12995869	-0.21	0.8373
time	-.8200195671	1.27227104	-0.64	0.5195
time*black	-.0617870014	0.14583481	-0.42	0.6720
time*hispanic	0.1051814604	0.16256679	0.65	0.5179
time*childage	0.2195306957	0.10734673	2.05	0.0413
time*married	-.1748734507	0.14921056	-1.17	0.2417
time*gender	0.1106505035	0.12583960	0.88	0.3796
time*momage	-.0441493754	0.02971813	-1.49	0.1379
time*momwork	-.1244505238	0.13269724	-0.94	0.3487

It's also worth noting that, like interactions in general, the interactions between time and the time-invariant covariates have a dual interpretation:

- The effect of the covariate varies with time.
- The effect of time varies with the level of the covariate.

Often the latter interpretation will be more compelling. For example, the coefficient of .219 for the CHILDAGE*TIME interaction says that with each one-year increase in age at time 1, the rate of change in antisocial behavior from time 1 to time 2 goes up by .219. That is, older children have a more rapid rate of increase.

2.4 Estimation with PROC GLM for More Than Two Observations Per Person

When each person has three or more measurements on the time-varying variables, it's not obvious how to extend the method of difference scores. One approach is to compute first-difference scores for each pair of adjacent observations, yielding $T - 1$ observations for each individual. Then the problem is to estimate a single model for the entire set while allowing for correlated errors.[1] Another approach is the dummy variable method, which gives the correct results in this new situation but is computationally intensive. In general, the easiest method is the one that was implemented in the last section using the ABSORB statement in PROC GLM. We now consider that method in greater detail.

---

[1] One reasonable method is to do generalized least squares on the difference equations, allowing for unrestricted correlations between the error terms from the same individual. In SAS, this can be done with PROC GENMOD using the REPEATED statement.

As before, our basic model is given by the equation

$$y_{it} = \mu_t + \beta x_{it} + \alpha_i + \varepsilon_{it} \qquad\qquad i = 1,\dots, n; \; t = 1,\dots, T$$

where α_i is a set of fixed parameters, ε_{it} satisfies the assumptions of a standard linear model and x_{it} is assumed to be strictly exogenous. OLS produces optimal estimates of the parameters, but direct application of OLS with dummy variables for the α_i terms is computationally tedious. It turns out, however, that we can get identical results by "conditioning out" the α_i terms and performing OLS on deviation scores. That is, for each person and for each time-varying variable (both response variables and predictors), we compute the means over time for that person:

$$\bar{y}_i = \frac{1}{n_i}\sum_t y_{it}$$

$$\bar{x}_i = \frac{1}{n_i}\sum_t x_{it}$$

where n_i is the number of measurements for person i. Then we subtract the person-specific means from the observed values of each variable:

$$y_{it}^* = y_{it} - \bar{y}_i$$
$$x_{it}^* = x_{it} - \bar{x}_i$$

Finally, we regress y^* on x^*, plus variables to represent the effect of time. This is what PROC GLM does when you use the ABSORB command.

If you construct the deviation scores yourself (using, say, PROC MEANS and a DATA step) and then use PROC REG to estimate the regression, you will get the correct OLS regression coefficients for the time-varying predictors. But the standard errors and p-values will be incorrect. That's because PROC REG calculates the degrees of freedom based on the number of variables on the MODEL statement, but it should actually include the number of dummy variables implicitly used to represent different persons in the sample (580 for the NLSY data). Formulas are available to correct these statistics (Judge et al. 1985), but it's much easier to let PROC GLM do it automatically. When the ABSORB statement is used, GLM converts all variables to deviation scores, estimates the regression, and uses the correct degrees of freedom to compute standard errors and p-values.

Let's try this with the NLSY data, except now we also include data from the middle year, 1992. Again, the first step is to construct a data set with one observation for each person at each time point:

```
DATA persyr3;
   SET my.nlsy;
   id=_N_;
   time=1;
   anti=anti90;
   self=self90;
   pov=pov90;
   OUTPUT;
```

```
        time=2;
        anti=anti92;
        self=self92;
        pov=pov92;
        OUTPUT;
        time=3;
        anti=anti94;
        self=self94;
        pov=pov94;
        OUTPUT;
RUN;
```

If there were more than three time points, it might be worthwhile to shorten this program by using arrays and a DO loop. Note that TIME has been assigned values of 1, 2 and 3, which facilitates the use of a CLASS statement in PROC GLM. This DATA step produced 1,743 observations, three for each of the 581 children.

The PROC GLM statements for estimating the basic model are virtually identical to those for the two-period case, except that we now use a CLASS statement to handle the three-valued TIME variable:

```
PROC GLM DATA=persyr3;
    ABSORB id;
    CLASS time;
    MODEL anti=self pov time / SOLUTION;
RUN;
```

Note that for this to work, the data set must be sorted by the variable specified on the ABSORB statement. Of course, the DATA step that produced PERSYR3 did this automatically.

Results in Output 2.10 are similar to what we found in Output 2.2 for two time points: a highly significant effect of self-esteem with a coefficient of about –.055, and a nonsignificant effect of poverty. TIME also has a significant effect, with antisocial behavior increasing over the three periods.

Output 2.10 GLM Estimates of a Fixed Effects Model for Three Periods

Dependent Variable: anti

Source	DF	Sum of Squares	Mean Square	F Value	Pr > F
Model	584	3181.883112	5.448430	5.48	<.0001
Error	1158	1151.232207	0.994156		
Corrected Total	1742	4333.115318			

R-Square	Coeff Var	Root MSE	anti Mean
0.734318	60.91480	0.997074	1.636833

continued

Output 2.10 *(continued)*

Source	DF	Type I SS	Mean Square	F Value	Pr > F
id	580	3142.448652	5.418015	5.45	<.0001
self	1	23.966255	23.966255	24.11	<.0001
pov	1	1.254392	1.254392	1.26	0.2615
time	2	14.213813	7.106907	7.15	0.0008

Source	DF	Type III SS	Mean Square	F Value	Pr > F
self	1	27.29362397	27.29362397	27.45	<.0001
pov	1	1.44138475	1.44138475	1.45	0.2288
time	2	14.21381348	7.10690674	7.15	0.0008

Parameter		Estimate	Standard Error	t Value	Pr > |t|
self		-.0551514027	0.01052575	-5.24	<.0001
pov		0.1124748908	0.09340988	1.20	0.2288
time	1	-.2107365666	0.05879781	-3.58	0.0004
time	2	-.1663431979	0.05856544	-2.84	0.0046
time	3	0.0000000000	.	.	.

We also learn from the output that 73% of the variation in antisocial behavior is *between* children, whereas the remaining 27% is *within* children (across time). I got these numbers by dividing the Type I sum of squares for ID (3142.44) by the corrected total sum of squares (4333.12), which yields .73. The square root of this number (.85) is an estimate of the intraclass correlation for these data. Since the total R^2 from the model is also .73, we conclude that the time-dependent predictors are not accounting for much additional variation.

It's also instructive to compare the results in Output 2.10 to what you get when the ABSORB command is omitted—that is, OLS regression with no control for between-person variation. These results are shown in Output 2.11. Notice first that the mean squared error in Output 2.10 is less than half of what we see in Output 2.11. That's because the control for between-person variation greatly reduces the error sum of squares (the R^2 increases from .048 to .734). It also reduces the degrees of freedom (which would make the mean squared error larger), but in this case, the reduction is not nearly as rapid. In data sets where the between-person proportion of variation in the dependent variable is small, the mean squared error could go up rather than down in a fixed effects model.

Output 2.11 Conventional OLS without Control for Between-Person Variation

Dependent Variable: anti

Source	DF	Sum of Squares	Mean Square	F Value	Pr > F
Model	4	208.312848	52.078212	21.94	<.0001
Error	1738	4124.802470	2.373304		
Corrected Total	1742	4333.115318			

R-Square	Coeff Var	Root MSE	anti Mean
0.048075	94.11792	1.540553	1.636833

Source	DF	Type III SS	Mean Square	F Value	Pr > F
self	1	86.3022527	86.3022527	36.36	<.0001
pov	1	102.8341414	102.8341414	43.33	<.0001
time	2	15.7786990	7.8893495	3.32	0.0362

Parameter		Estimate	Standard Error	t Value	Pr > |t|
Intercept		2.959617390	0.23985318	12.34	<.0001
self		-0.066894066	0.01109311	-6.03	<.0001
pov		0.517573842	0.07862856	6.58	<.0001
time	1	-0.222741659	0.09059359	-2.46	0.0140
time	2	-0.172135548	0.09043193	-1.90	0.0571
time	3	0.000000000	.	.	.

The root mean squared error directly affects the standard errors of the coefficients, so we might expect the standard errors to be smaller for the fixed effects regression than for the conventional regression. That's true for SELF, where the fixed effects standard error is .0105 while the conventional OLS standard error is .0111. But for POV, the fixed effects standard error is .0934 and the conventional OLS standard error is .0786. Why the difference? The answer is that the standard errors depend not only on the root mean square error, but also on the relative proportion of within- and between-person variation on the predictor variables. Other things being equal, the greater the proportion of variation that is between persons on a given predictor variable, the larger the standard error of its fixed effects coefficient. Other analysis shows that for SELF, 53% of the variation is between persons. For POV, on the other hand, the between-person variation is 70%. That's why the standard error for POV went up rather than down under the fixed effects analysis. The ideal situation for a fixed effects analysis is when all of the variation on the time-varying predictors is within persons, but there's still lots of between-person variation on the response variable.

As in the two-period case, we can also test whether the time-varying predictors have coefficients that vary with time by including interactions between them and TIME:

```
PROC GLM DATA=persyr3;
    ABSORB id;
    CLASS time;
    MODEL anti=self pov time self*time pov*time / SOLUTION;
RUN;
```

With high *p*-values for the two interactions, Output 2.12 shows no evidence for variation over time of the coefficients for SELF and POV.

Output 2.12 Tests for Interaction between TIME and Time-Varying Predictors

Source	DF	Type III SS	Mean Square	F Value	Pr > F
self	1	26.61340572	26.61340572	26.74	<.0001
pov	1	1.34058714	1.34058714	1.35	0.2460
time	2	3.72428319	1.86214160	1.87	0.1544
self*time	2	2.62684393	1.31342197	1.32	0.2676
pov*time	2	0.04291216	0.02145608	0.02	0.9787

In a similar way, we can test for constancy of the effects of time-invariant predictors:

```
PROC GLM DATA=persyr3;
    ABSORB id;
    CLASS time;
    MODEL anti=self pov time black*time hispanic*time
        childage*time married*time gender*time
        momage*time momwork*time / SOLUTION;
RUN;
```

As shown in Output 2.13, there is no evidence that any of the time-invariant predictors has an effect that varies with time.

Output 2.13 Tests for Interaction between TIME and Time-Invariant Predictors

Source	DF	Type III SS	Mean Square	F Value	Pr > F
self	1	24.13352368	24.13352368	24.41	<.0001
pov	1	1.28045845	1.28045845	1.30	0.2553
time	2	0.48255089	0.24127545	0.24	0.7835
black*time	2	4.99285922	2.49642961	2.53	0.0805
hispanic*time	2	1.63509176	0.81754588	0.83	0.4376
childage*time	2	5.06884670	2.53442335	2.56	0.0774
married*time	2	1.21443928	0.60721964	0.61	0.5412

continued

Output 2.13 *(continued)*

Source	DF	Type III SS	Mean Square	F Value	Pr > F
gender*time	2	0.94702064	0.47351032	0.48	0.6195
momage*time	2	2.77934289	1.38967145	1.41	0.2456
momwork*time	2	3.47491248	1.73745624	1.76	0.1729

In addition to PROC GLM, another SAS procedure, PROC TSCSREG (for time series cross section regression), also does OLS estimation of the fixed effects model. PROC TSCSREG, which is a component of the ETS product, has one nice feature that I will discuss in the next section, a Hausman test of fixed effects versus random effects. However, the downside of PROC TSCSREG is that it explicitly estimates coefficients for the dummy variables for the fixed effects and thus may use excessive computer time for large samples.

2.5 Fixed Effects versus Random Effects

It should come as no surprise to learn that fixed effects methods are not the only way to estimate regression models for longitudinal data. There are several popular alternatives, many of which are readily available in SAS. To fully appreciate both the strengths and weaknesses of the fixed effects method, we need to compare it with some of these alternatives.

The closest cousin to the fixed effects model is the random effects or mixed model. We start with the same basic equation:

$$y_{it} = \mu_t + \beta x_{it} + \gamma z_i + \alpha_i + \varepsilon_{it} \qquad i = 1,\ldots, n; t = 1,\ldots, T \qquad (2.5)$$

Now, however, instead of assuming that α_i represents a set of fixed parameters, we suppose that each α_i is a random variable with a specified probability distribution. Typically, it is assumed that α_i has a normal distribution with a mean of 0 and constant variance, and that it's independent of z_i, x_{it}, and ε_{it}.

This random effects model can be readily estimated with PROC MIXED:

```
PROC MIXED DATA=persyr3 COVTEST NOCLPRINT;
   CLASS id time;
   MODEL anti=pov self time / SOLUTION;
   RANDOM INTERCEPT / SUBJECT=id;
RUN;
```

The COVTEST option requests a test statistic for the null hypothesis that the variance of $\alpha_i =$ 0. NOCLPRINT suppresses printing of the values of the CLASS variables (581 values for ID). The RANDOM statement is what introduces the person-level random component into the regression model.[2] Here it says that the intercept is a random variable that differs for

---

[2] The same results can be obtained with the following statement:
```
RANDOM id;
```
However, with this statement, the computing time increases by a factor of about 20.

each value of the ID variable. Without the RANDOM statement, PROC MIXED would produce the same OLS estimates as in Output 2.11.

Results are shown in Output 2.14. The first panel—labeled "Covariance Parameter Estimates"—gives estimates of the variances of α_i (labeled "Intercept") and ε_t (labeled "Residual"). Both variances are significantly greater than 0. The regression coefficients in the lower panel are closer to the conventional OLS estimates in Output 2.11 than they are to the fixed effects estimates in Output 2.10. Most importantly, the coefficient for POV is highly significant in the random effects model, but didn't even approach significance in the fixed effects model.

Output 2.14 Random Effects Model with Time-Varying Predictors

Covariance Parameter Estimates

Cov Parm	Subject	Estimate	Standard Error	Z Value	Pr Z
Intercept	id	1.3875	0.1025	13.54	<.0001
Residual		0.9971	0.04152	24.01	<.0001

Solution for Fixed Effects

Effect	time	Estimate	Standard Error	DF	t Value	Pr > |t|
Intercept		2.8832	0.2085	580	13.83	<.0001
pov		0.2947	0.07745	1158	3.81	0.0001
self		-0.05971	0.009533	1158	-6.26	<.0001
time	1	-0.2157	0.05883	1158	-3.67	0.0003
time	2	-0.1688	0.05864	1158	-2.88	0.0041
time	3	0	.	.	.	.

Why the difference between fixed and random effects estimates? The main reason is that, unlike the fixed effects model, the random effects model does not really control for between-person variation. That's because a key assumption of the method is that α_i is uncorrelated with x_{it}. The fixed effects model, on the other hand, imposes no restrictions on the relationship between α_i and x_{it}.

So what good is the random effects model? Well, it's better than conventional OLS because the standard error estimates adjust for the within-person correlation in the repeated measurements of the dependent variable. By contrast, conventional OLS standard errors are biased downward by the dependence in the multiple observations for each person. But that advantage is also shared with the fixed effects estimator.

One thing that the random effects method can do that the fixed effects method cannot is produce coefficient estimates for time-invariant variables. For example, Output 2.15 shows the results of adding seven time-invariant predictors to the random effects model we just fitted. Only two of them, GENDER and MOMWORK, are statistically significant at the .05 level. The coefficients for POV and SELF don't change much by the addition of these variables. Neither does the estimate of the variance of α_i, which would be expected to decline with the addition of strong, person-specific predictors to the model. Keep in mind that the fixed effects model also controls for these time-invariant predictors; it just doesn't produce coefficient estimates for them. Furthermore, unlike the random effects method, it controls for *all* time-invariant predictors, not just those that have been measured and included in the regression model.

Output 2.15 Random Effects Model with Time-Varying and Time-Invariant Predictors

Covariance Parameter Estimates

Cov Parm	Subject	Estimate	Standard Error	Z Value	Pr Z
Intercept	id	1.3056	0.09810	13.31	<.0001
Residual		0.9959	0.04144	24.03	<.0001

Solution for Fixed Effects

Effect	time	Estimate	Standard Error	DF	t Value	Pr > |t|
Intercept		2.7471	1.0985	573	2.50	0.0127
pov		0.2460	0.08038	1158	3.06	0.0023
self		-0.06201	0.009512	1158	-6.52	<.0001
time	1	-0.2163	0.05879	1158	-3.68	0.0002
time	2	-0.1690	0.05860	1158	-2.88	0.0040
time	3	0	.	.	.	.
black		0.2271	0.1259	1158	1.80	0.0715
hispanic		-0.2180	0.1385	1158	-1.57	0.1156
childage		0.08846	0.09125	1158	0.97	0.3325
married		-0.04933	0.1266	1158	-0.39	0.6970
gender		-0.4834	0.1067	1158	-4.53	<.0001
momage		-0.02195	0.02533	1158	-0.87	0.3864
momwork		0.2614	0.1149	1158	2.28	0.0231

Another attractive feature of the random effects model is the ability to introduce random coefficients for the time-varying predictors. For example, we can rewrite the model as

$$y_{it} = \mu_t + \beta_i x_{it} + \gamma z_i + \alpha_i + \varepsilon_{it}$$

which simply puts an *i* subscript on the β coefficient. We then assume that β_i is a set of normally distributed random variables with a common mean and variance, both of which can be estimated. We also assume that β_i is independent of x_{it}, ε_{it} and z_i (but could possibly covary with α_i).

For the NLSY data, let's consider a model that allows the effect of POV to vary randomly across children. Here is the SAS code:[3]

```
PROC MIXED DATA=persyr3 COVTEST NOCLPRINT;
    CLASS id time;
    MODEL anti=pov self time / SOLUTION;
    RANDOM INTERCEPT pov / SUBJECT=id;
RUN;
```

Results are shown in Output 2.16. As shown in the first panel, the estimate of the variance of the POV coefficient is .2317. The z-test for the null hypothesis that this variance is 0 has a p-value of .0509. So there is only marginal evidence for non-zero variation in the coefficient across persons.[4] In the "Solution for Fixed Effects" panel, the estimate for POV of .3053 can be regarded as an estimate of the average effect of this variable.

Output 2.16 Random Effects Model with Random Coefficient

Covariance Parameter Estimates

Cov Parm	Subject	Estimate	Standard Error	Z Value	Pr Z
Intercept	id	1.3261	0.1064	12.47	<.0001
pov	id	0.2317	0.1416	1.64	0.0509
Residual		0.9767	0.04236	23.05	<.0001

Solution for Fixed Effects

Effect	time	Estimate	Standard Error	DF	t Value	Pr > |t|
Intercept		2.8698	0.2083	580	13.77	<.0001
pov		0.3053	0.08204	170	3.72	0.0003
self		-0.05939	0.009536	988	-6.23	<.0001
time	1	-0.2154	0.05892	988	-3.66	0.0003
time	2	-0.1660	0.05859	988	-2.83	0.0047
time	3	0	.	.	.	.

---

[3] The same results can be obtained with the following statement
```
RANDOM id pov*id;
```
But this results in an enormous increase in computing time. Also, some might prefer to use the TYPE=UN option on the RANDOM statement. This allows for a covariance between the random intercept and the random slope.

[4] A more accurate test is computed by taking differences in $-2 \times$ log-likelihood for this model and the earlier model that forces the variance to be 0. However, correct calculation of this statistic also requires that the option METHOD=ML be used in the PROC statement for both models. (The default method is REML, i.e., restricted maximum likelihood). When I did this calculation, the resulting chi-square statistic was 3.0 with 1 d.f., giving a p-value of .08.

There are many other possible variations on random effects models. For example, besides having a random effect for persons, one could also have random effects for higher levels of aggregation such as families or schools (assuming that the data contain multiple persons for each family or school). PROC MIXED also allows for autoregressive and other covariance structures on the ε_{it} component.

None of these elaborations allows the random effects model to control for all possible time-invariant predictors, as the fixed effects model does. On the other hand, if there is really no correlation between α_i and x_{it}—that is, between the person-specific effect and the time-varying predictors—then random effects estimates might have far less sampling variability than the fixed effects estimates. That translates into more powerful hypothesis tests and narrower confidence intervals. The reason is that the random effects method uses variation both within persons and between persons, whereas the fixed effects method uses only variation within persons.

Mundlak (1978) has argued that the random effects method should be seen as a special case of the fixed effects method. In a nutshell, the argument goes like this. We start with a conventional random effects model such as equation (2.5), and then relax its restrictions by allowing for all possible correlations between the random component and the time-varying predictors. When this is done, ML estimates of the random effects model become identical to the OLS estimates for the fixed effects model. In general, whenever one has a choice between two nested models, one being a restricted version of the other, there is a tradeoff between bias and efficiency. The more parsimonious model (the random effects model in this case) will lead to more efficient estimates, but those estimates might be biased if the restrictions of the model are incorrect. The less parsimonious model (the fixed effects model) is less prone to bias, but at the expense of greater sampling variability.

It would be nice to have a statistical test of the random effects model against the fixed effects model as an alternative. That way we would have some basis for deciding whether we can tolerate the biases inherent in the random effects method, or whether we need to go with the less restrictive fixed effects model. One such test is available in PROC TSCSREG. When you ask this procedure to estimate a random effects model, it automatically reports a Hausman test (Greene 2000, p. 576), which compares the fixed effects and random effects models.[5]

The PROC TSCSREG code for the NLSY data follows immediately. Note that TSCSREG does not have a CLASS statement, so it's necessary to create dummy variables for TIME in a DATA step. TSCSREG expects the data to be sorted by person, and within person by time. The ID statement tells TSCSREG what variables index these two dimensions. In the MODEL statement, the RANONE option is what specifies a random effects model. Changing this to FIXONE would produce a fixed effects model. As noted earlier, however, the downside of this PROC is that the coefficients for the dummy variables in the fixed

---

[5] The Hausman test is computed as follows. Let **b** be the vector of fixed effects coefficients (excluding the constant) and let β be the vector of random effects coefficients. Let $\Sigma = \text{var}(\mathbf{b}) - \text{var}(\beta)$ where $\text{var}(\mathbf{b})$ is the estimated covariance matrix for **b** and similarly for β. The statistic is then $m = (\mathbf{b} - \beta)'\Sigma^{-1}(\mathbf{b} - \beta)$, which has a chi-square distribution under the null hypothesis.

effects model are explicitly estimated and reported, requiring lots of computer time and excessive output. Another disadvantage is that TSCSREG requires that the data be balanced—each person must have the same number of observations. PROC GLM and PROC MIXED, on the other hand, can handle unbalanced data sets without difficulty.

Here's the code:

```
DATA tscset;
    SET persyr3;
    time1=(time=1);
    time2=(time=2);
PROC TSCSREG DATA=tscset;
    ID id time;
    MODEL anti=self pov time1 time2 / RANONE;
RUN;
```

Results in Output 2.17 are virtually identical to what we got with PROC MIXED in Output 2.14. But we also get the "Hausman Test for Random Effects," which tests the null hypothesis of the random effects model against the alternative fixed effects model. In this case, the low *p*-value indicates that the random effects model should be rejected. While the Hausman test can be very useful, it is also somewhat ad hoc and can break down entirely in certain circumstances (the Σ matrix in note 5 may not be positive definite). In chapter 6 we shall see how to construct a likelihood ratio statistic for the same null hypothesis.

Output 2.17 TSCSREG Output for Random Effects Model with Hausman Test

Variance Component Estimates	
Variance Component for Cross Sections	1.380509
Variance Component for Error	0.994156

Hausman Test for Random Effects		
DF	m Value	Pr > m
2	12.82	0.0016

Parameter Estimates					
Variable	DF	Estimate	Standard Error	t Value	Pr > |t|
Intercept	1	2.883232	0.2085	13.83	<.0001
self	1	-0.05971	0.00953	-6.26	<.0001
pov	1	0.294928	0.0775	3.81	0.0001
time1	1	-0.21575	0.0588	-3.67	0.0003
time2	1	-0.16877	0.0587	-2.88	0.0041

Another approach that is closely related to the random effects method is generalized estimating equations (GEE), which can be implemented with PROC GENMOD. In the case of linear models, GEE is equivalent to generalized least squares, which also happens to be the default method used in PROC TSCSREG. GEE makes no explicit assumptions about person-specific random components in the regression model. It simply allows for correlations in the dependent variable across observations (over time in this case).

For the NLSY data, the GEE method can be used to estimate the random effects model by specifying the following in PROC GENMOD:

```
PROC GENMOD DATA=persyr3;
   CLASS id time;
   MODEL anti= self pov time;
   REPEATED SUBJECT=id / TYPE=EXCH MODELSE;
RUN;
```

The REPEATED statement invokes GEE estimation. The TYPE=EXCH option specifies that correlations between measurements of ANTI in different years are all equal. This is the correlation structure that is implied by a simple random effects model such as equation (2.5). MODELSE specifies that standard errors are calculated based on the assumed model rather than using the default method of robust standard errors.

In Output 2.18, we see that the "Exchangeable Working Correlation" is .58. This is an estimate of the correlation between error terms in different years; because we specified the EXCH option, these are identical for all pairs of years. Parameter estimates and associated statistics in Output 2.18 are virtually identical to those in Outputs 2.17 and 2.14. It's worth noting that GENMOD is by far the most computationally efficient procedure for getting these random effects parameter estimates. On my PC, PROC MIXED took .23 seconds, PROC TSCSREG took .75 seconds, and PROC GENMOD took 0.15 seconds. (In fairness to MIXED, if the model is specified using the REPEATED statement rather than the RANDOM statement, the time can be reduced to 0.09 seconds).

Output 2.18 GEE Estimates of Random Effects Model

Exchangeable Working Correlation	
Correlation	0.5819870399

Analysis Of GEE Parameter Estimates

Model-Based Standard Error Estimates

Parameter		Estimate	Standard Error	95% Confidence Limits		Z	Pr > |Z|
Intercept		2.8832	0.2085	2.4745	3.2918	13.83	<.0001
self		-0.0597	0.0095	-0.0784	-0.0410	-6.26	<.0001
pov		0.2947	0.0775	0.1429	0.4465	3.80	0.0001
time	1	-0.2157	0.0588	-0.3310	-0.1004	-3.67	0.0002
time	2	-0.1688	0.0586	-0.2837	-0.0538	-2.88	0.0040
time	3	0.0000	0.0000	0.0000	0.0000	.	.
Scale		1.5444	.	.	.	.	.

Somewhat different results are obtained in Output 2.19 when the REPEATED statement is altered to read as follows:

```
REPEATED SUBJECT=id / TYPE=UN CORRW;
```

TYPE=UN specifies an unstructured correlation matrix, which is reflected in the different correlations seen in the working correlation matrix (requested with the CORRW option). I've also omitted the MODELSE option, thereby asking GENMOD to compute robust standard errors using White's (1980) method. Both of these changes should make the results somewhat less sensitive to misspecification of the error structure. The parameter estimates and associated statistics are all a bit different from those estimated under the random effects model, but still quite similar.

Output 2.19 GEE Estimates for a Less Restricted Model

Working Correlation Matrix

	Col1	*Col2*	*Col3*
Row1	1.0000	0.5785	0.5359
Row2	0.5785	1.0000	0.6396
Row3	0.5359	0.6396	1.0000

Analysis Of GEE Parameter Estimates

Empirical Standard Error Estimates

Parameter		*Estimate*	*Standard Error*	*95% Confidence Limits*		*Z*	*Pr > |Z|*
Intercept		2.8935	0.2322	2.4384	3.3485	12.46	<.0001
self		-0.0605	0.0102	-0.0805	-0.0405	-5.93	<.0001
pov		0.3140	0.0812	0.1549	0.4730	3.87	0.0001
time	1	-0.2164	0.0636	-0.3410	-0.0918	-3.40	0.0007
time	2	-0.1691	0.0594	-0.2855	-0.0527	-2.85	0.0044
time	3	0.0000	0.0000	0.0000	0.0000	.	.

2.6 A Hybrid Method

As we've seen, both the GEE method and the random effects method may produce estimates that are markedly different from the fixed effects estimates. That's because neither of those methods controls for stable, unmeasured characteristics of the individuals. There's another approach, however, that combines some of the virtues of fixed effects and random effects methods. This method produces coefficient estimates that are identical to those from the fixed effects method, but the standard errors and test statistics might be somewhat different, depending on the details of the estimation method.

The basic idea is to decompose the time-varying predictors into two parts, one representing within-person variation, the other representing between-person variation (Neuhaus and Kalbfleisch 1998). Both of these components are used as predictors in the regression model. The coefficients for the within-person components will be identical to those for the classic fixed effects estimates.

There are several potential advantages of doing it this way. One is that you also get estimates for the between-person effects, as well as coefficients for any measured time-invariant predictors. Second, by testing whether the between-person coefficients are the same as the corresponding within-person coefficients, you get a test that has the same function as the Hausman test that we looked at earlier. That is, it can tell you whether a fixed effects approach offers any gains over a random effects regression. Third, using the options available in PROC MIXED, you can extend the conventional fixed effects models in several important ways.

Here's how to do it for the NLSY data. First, we use PROC MEANS to calculate the means for SELF and POV across the three observations for each child, and output them to a data set. The NWAY and NOPRINT options suppress unwanted output. The CLASS statement says to compute the means separately for each value of the ID variable. The data set of means is then merged with the original data, and deviations of each variable from its within-person mean are calculated:

```
PROC MEANS DATA=persyr3 NWAY NOPRINT;
   CLASS id;
   VAR self pov;
   OUTPUT OUT=a MEAN=mself mpov;
PROC SORT DATA=persyr3;
   BY id;
PROC SORT DATA=a;
   BY id;
DATA combine;
   MERGE persyr3 a;
   BY id;
   dself=self-mself;
   dpov=pov-mpov;
   dtime=time-2;
   time1=(time=1);
   time2=(time=2);
RUN;
```

Note that I've calculated deviation scores for TIME, although I won't use those in the first few models. (The mean of TIME is necessarily 2 for every child). I've also created two dummy variables, TIME1 and TIME2, so that I can represent time in PROC REG, which doesn't have a CLASS statement.

In the literature on multilevel models (Bryk and Raudenbusch 1992; Goldstein 1987; Kreft et al. 1995), the practice of subtracting person-specific means from each time-varying variable is referred to as *group-mean centering*. Although it is well-known that using group-mean centered variables can produce substantially different results, this literature has not generally made the connection to fixed effects models nor has it been recognized that group-mean centering controls for all time-invariant covariates.

The calculation of centered predictors is similar to the computational method for getting fixed effects estimates that I described in the previous section. What's new here is that we don't calculate centered scores for the *dependent* variable. Once the new data set is constructed, we can run an OLS regression with both the centered variables and the mean variables, along with any other time-invariant predictors that we want to include:

```
PROC REG DATA=combine;
   MODEL anti=dpov dself mpov mself time1 time2 black hispanic
         childage married gender momage momwork;
RUN;
```

Results are in Output 2.20. The coefficients for the centered variables, DPOV and DSELF, are the same as the fixed effects coefficients for POV and SELF in Output 2.10. But we also get coefficients for several time-invariant predictors, something that was not available with the earlier method.

Output 2.20 OLS Regression Using Centered Predictors

Root MSE	1.50725	R-Square	0.0935
Dependent Mean	1.63683	Adj R-Sq	0.0867
Coeff Var	92.08316		

Variable	DF	Parameter Estimate	Standard Error	t Value	Pr > |t|
Intercept	1	3.11882	0.79422	3.93	<.0001
dpov	1	0.11247	0.14121	0.80	0.4258
dself	1	-0.05515	0.01591	-3.47	0.0005
mpov	1	0.61643	0.10710	5.76	<.0001
mself	1	-0.09003	0.01506	-5.98	<.0001
time1	1	-0.21074	0.08888	-2.37	0.0179
time2	1	-0.16634	0.08853	-1.88	0.0604
black	1	0.11093	0.09019	1.23	0.2189
hispanic	1	-0.27990	0.09513	-2.94	0.0033
childage	1	0.08575	0.06206	1.38	0.1672
married	1	-0.12841	0.08788	-1.46	0.1441
gender	1	-0.50816	0.07289	-6.97	<.0001
momage	1	-0.01134	0.01738	-0.65	0.5142
momwork	1	0.16412	0.08141	2.02	0.0440

Despite the fact that the coefficients for DPOV and DSELF replicate our earlier results, the reported standard errors for those coefficients are about 50% larger in Output 2.20 than they were in Output 2.10. This means, of course, that the *t*-statistics are about 1/3 smaller. That's because the error term in the earlier regression consisted entirely of within-person variation on the dependent variable. Here there is both within-person and between-person variation. We can correct the problem by estimating a random effects model in PROC MIXED:

```
PROC MIXED DATA=combine COVTEST NOCLPRINT;
   CLASS id time;
   MODEL anti=dpov dself mpov mself time black hispanic
         childage married gender momage momwork / SOLUTION;
   RANDOM INTERCEPT / SUBJECT=id;
RUN;
```

Results in Output 2.21 have standard errors for DPOV and DSELF that are identical to those in Output 2.10. Note, however, that for the time-invariant predictors, the random effects standard errors are *larger* than the OLS standard errors rather than smaller (which is just what is expected from clustering adjustments).

Output 2.21 PROC MIXED Estimates for Centered Predictors

Covariance Parameter Estimates

Cov Parm	Subject	Estimate	Standard Error	Z Value	Pr Z
Intercept	id	1.2896	0.09692	13.31	<.0001
Residual		0.9942	0.04132	24.06	<.0001

Solution for Fixed Effects

Effect	time	Estimate	Standard Error	DF	t Value	Pr > |t|
Intercept		3.1188	1.1601	571	2.69	0.0074
dpov		0.1125	0.09341	1158	1.20	0.2288
dself		-0.05515	0.01053	1158	-5.24	<.0001
mpov		0.6164	0.1567	1158	3.93	<.0001
mself		-0.09003	0.02203	1158	-4.09	<.0001
time	1	-0.2107	0.05880	1158	-3.58	0.0004
time	2	-0.1663	0.05857	1158	-2.84	0.0046
time	3	0	.	.	.	.
black		0.1109	0.1320	1158	0.84	0.4007
hispanic		-0.2799	0.1392	1158	-2.01	0.0446
childage		0.08575	0.09080	1158	0.94	0.3452
married		-0.1284	0.1286	1158	-1.00	0.3181
gender		-0.5082	0.1066	1158	-4.77	<.0001
momage		-0.01134	0.02543	1158	-0.45	0.6558
momwork		0.1641	0.1191	1158	1.38	0.1685

What we've gained by the centering method is the ability to estimate coefficients for time-invariant predictors. It's essential to keep in mind, however, that the coefficients of the time invariant predictors (unlike those for the within-person time-varying predictors) will be biased if those variables are correlated with the unobserved fixed effects. There's another attraction to this approach. If the random effects model is correct (that is, if the time-varying predictors are uncorrelated with person-specific fixed effects), the coefficients for the centered variables should be the same as the coefficients for the mean variables. Since both are estimated in the same model, it's easy to test that assumption in PROC MIXED by including CONTRAST statements after the MODEL statement:

```
CONTRAST 'pov' dpov 1 mpov -1;
CONTRAST 'self' dself 1 mself -1;
CONTRAST 'overall' dpov 1 mpov -1, dself 1 mself -1;
```

For each CONTRAST statement, the text in quotes is a required label, used for distinguishing one test from another in the output. The first CONTRAST statement tests whether the coefficients for DPOV and MPOV are the same. In detail, the coefficient for DPOV is multiplied by 1, the coefficient for MPOV is multiplied by –1, the results are added together, and the sum is tested for a difference with 0. The next CONTRAST statement does the same for the two self-esteem variables, and the final CONTRAST statement tests both hypotheses simultaneously. In Output 2.22, we see strong evidence that the assumption is not satisfied for POV, but might be for SELF. The overall test yields results very similar to the Hausman test in Output 2.17.

Output 2.22 Tests for Fixed Effects vs. Random Effects Using Centered Scores

	Contrasts			
Label	Num DF	Den DF	F Value	Pr > F
pov	1	1158	7.63	0.0058
self	1	1158	2.04	0.1535
overall	2	1158	4.93	0.0073

If we conclude that the coefficients for the mean and deviation scores are different for a particular variable, a natural question is whether the coefficient for the mean has any useful interpretation. In most cases, I don't think so, because that coefficient is typically confounded with the effects of other unobserved variables. Nevertheless, it's important to have the mean variables in the model in order to get good estimates of the effects of other time-invariant variables. Omitting them would mean that the variable in question was not fully controlled.

Another advantage of the centering method for getting fixed effects estimates is that we can allow for random variation in the slope parameters for the time-varying predictors. For example, instead of estimating separate coefficients for time 1 and time 2, let's assume that the antisocial behavior changes linearly with time. Then we allow the coefficient of TIME (actually DTIME, which is TIME minus the mean of 2) to vary randomly from child to child—a random, linear growth model. Here's how to set it up:

```
PROC MIXED DATA=combine COVTEST NOCLPRINT;
   CLASS id;
   MODEL anti=dpov dself dtime mpov mself / SOLUTION;
   RANDOM INTERCEPT dtime / SUBJECT=id;
RUN;
```

Output 2.23 gives the results. We see that the fixed coefficient for DTIME (.1055) is highly significant, but the variance around that coefficient (.1409) is also highly significant. So we conclude that antisocial behavior tends to increase over time during the adolescent years, but there is substantial variation among children in the rate of increase.

Output 2.23 Estimates for a Random Growth Curve Model with Fixed Effects

Covariance Parameter Estimates

Cov Parm	Subject	Estimate	Standard Error	Z Value	Pr Z
Intercept	id	1.4139	0.1013	13.96	<.0001
dtime	id	0.1409	0.04184	3.37	0.0004
Residual		0.8539	0.05021	17.01	<.0001

Solution for Fixed Effects

Effect	Estimate	Standard Error	DF	t Value	Pr > |t|
Intercept	2.9336	0.4616	579	6.36	<.0001
dpov	0.1387	0.09391	578	1.48	0.1402
dself	-0.05515	0.01048	578	-5.26	<.0001
dtime	0.1055	0.03140	580	3.36	0.0008
mpov	0.6842	0.1376	578	4.97	<.0001
mself	-0.07477	0.02225	578	-3.36	0.0008

In the same way, I tried fitting models for random variation in the effect of POV and SELF, but there is no evidence for such variation (results not shown). This approach of combining models with fixed and random effects is quite similar to the conditional linear mixed models of Verbeke et al. (2001), although they used a somewhat different computational method for obtaining the estimates.[6]

One final attraction of estimating the fixed effects model with PROC MIXED is the ability to specify models for the error structure that are less constrained than the conventional fixed effects method, which implies a covariance structure for the dependent variable known as

---

[6] Verbeke et al. (2001) provide a SAS macro that transforms the data set as a precursor to using PROC MIXED.

compound symmetry. Compound symmetry means that variance of the error term is constant over time and the covariance between any two time points is the same. PROC MIXED allows for a wide variety of alternative structures that can be specified with the REPEATED statement. Although there isn't space for a detailed discussion of the many options, let's consider the most general option, which has no constraints whatever on the error structure. While this option would not work well if there were many time points (there would be too many different covariances), it's quite reasonable when there are only three. A model with an unstructured covariance matrix is specified as follows:

```
PROC MIXED DATA=combine COVTEST NOCLPRINT;
   CLASS id time;
   MODEL anti=dpov dself mpov mself time black hispanic
         childage married gender momage momwork / SOLUTION;
   REPEATED time / SUBJECT=id TYPE=UN;
RUN;
```

On the REPEATED statement, the TIME variable is optional as long as everyone has the same number of time points and they are in the same order. UN stands for unstructured. The output from this program (not shown) has both coefficients and standard errors that differ slightly from those in Output 2.23, but with no appreciable change in the p-values.[7]

2.7 An Example with Unbalanced Data

In the NLSY example, the data set was *balanced* with exactly three observations for every child. But the fixed effects method is by no means limited to balanced data; it can be applied without modification to data in which some persons have many observations and others have few. Persons with only one observation, however, are effectively eliminated from the analysis because such individuals have no within-person variation.

In this section I apply the fixed effects method to a highly unbalanced data set in which the "individuals" are schools and the "occasions" are students within each school. The National Education Longitudinal Study (NELS) began in 1988 and included 1,003 schools with a total 21,580 students. Schools varied widely in the number of their students who were interviewed, ranging from 1 to 67. The version of the data set I use here is described in Kreft and De Leeuw (1998) and is available on the Internet (http://www.stat.ucla.edu/~deleeuw/sagebook/). Only data from the 1988 interview are used here.

The dependent variable MATHSCOR is the number of items correct on a mathematics achievement test. Our goal is to estimate a regression model with the following predictor variables:

SEX   1 = female, 0 = male

ASIAN   1 = Asian, otherwise 0

HISPANIC   1 = Hispanic, regardless of race, otherwise 0

---

[7] Another, similar approach is to modify the program that produced Output 2.23 by specifying the EMPIRICAL option on the PROC statement. This produces robust standard errors and test statistics using the method of White (1980), which allows for heterogeneous variances and unstructured correlations.

BLACK   1 = Black and not Hispanic, otherwise 0

HOMEWORK Hours per week spent on homework

SES   Socioeconomic status (ranges from –2.5 to 2.3)

PARED   Parent's education, measured on a scale ranging from 1 to 6

The omitted category for the set of race and ethnicity dummy variables is White (not of Hispanic origin).

I first estimate a conventional linear regression model using PROC GLM:

```
PROC GLM DATA=my.nels88;
   MODEL mathscor=sex black hispanic asian amerind
        homework ses pared;
   RUN;
```

This code produces the results shown in Output 2.24. Given the large sample size, it's not surprising to find that all the coefficients are statistically significant at any conventional level. But there are two potential problems here. First, the standard errors might be underestimated because there is no correction for dependence within schools. Second, there is no control for school-level variables that might be correlated with the individual characteristics, and thus coefficient estimates might be biased.

Output 2.24 Conventional Regression Estimates with PROC GLM

R-Square	Coeff Var	Root MSE	mathscor Mean
0.302480	16.67138	8.504799	51.01436

Parameter	Estimate	Standard Error	t Value	Pr > |t|
Intercept	46.52654032	0.30199113	154.07	<.0001
sex	0.49744862	0.11600764	4.29	<.0001
black	-5.23792860	0.19008579	-27.56	<.0001
hispanic	-2.86035498	0.18657937	-15.33	<.0001
asian	1.76632831	0.24881195	7.10	<.0001
amerind	-4.64928956	0.53671967	-8.66	<.0001
homework	1.29760317	0.04026601	32.23	<.0001
ses	3.72086392	0.14611981	25.46	<.0001
pared	0.86267418	0.08794691	9.81	<.0001

Both of these difficulties are addressed by the use of the fixed effects method, implemented here by using PROC GLM with the ABSORB statement:

```
PROC GLM DATA=my.nels88;
   ABSORB schoolid;
   MODEL mathscor=sex black hispanic asian amerind
        homework ses pared;
   RUN;
```

Results are shown in Output 2.25.

Output 2.25 Fixed Effects Analysis with PROC GLM

R-Square	Coeff Var	Root MSE	mathscor Mean
0.396666	15.87818	8.100153	51.01436

Parameter	Estimate	Standard Error	t Value	Pr > |t|
sex	0.513893601	0.11495955	4.47	<.0001
black	-3.757158700	0.24154883	-15.55	<.0001
hispanic	-1.768794279	0.22738925	-7.78	<.0001
asian	1.903077171	0.26397493	7.21	<.0001
amerind	-2.973568213	0.56610286	-5.25	<.0001
homework	1.181563760	0.04080071	28.96	<.0001
ses	2.818123661	0.15095592	18.67	<.0001
pared	0.589485288	0.08719577	6.76	<.0001

Although all the coefficients are still statistically significant under the fixed effects method, there are some notable differences between Output 2.24 and Output 2.25. The coefficients for BLACK, HISPANIC and AMERIND (all of which are comparisons with White) have declined substantially in magnitude. Furthermore, the standard errors for BLACK and HISPANIC have increased, with the result that the *t*-statistics for these variables are much lower than they were in Output 2.23. The coefficients for SES and PARED (but not their standard errors) have also declined substantially.

The degree to which the coefficients change under fixed effects estimation as compared with conventional OLS appears to be related to the degree of between- versus within-school variation on the predictor variables. For each variable, here is the proportion of variation that is between schools:

SEX   .08
BLACK   .44
HISPANIC   .39
ASIAN   .17
AMERIND   .17
HOMEWORK   .14
SES   .42
PARED   .34

It is apparent that those predictor variables with little between-school variation showed little change in coefficients or standard errors under the fixed effects method.

These proportions were obtained by fitting a separate fixed effects model for each of the variables. Each variable was treated as the dependent variable, but no predictor variables were specified. For example,

```
PROC GLM DATA=my.nels88;
   ABSORB schoolid;
   MODEL pared=;
RUN;
```

The proportion of variation that is between schools is just the R^2 from this regression.

Another change is that the R^2 has noticeably increased, from .30 in Output 2.24 to .40 in Output 2.25. We can test for the significance of this increase by computing

$$\frac{(.39666 - .30248)/1002}{(1 - .39666)/20569} = 3.20$$

Under the null hypothesis of no school effects (net of other variables), this statistic has an F distribution with 1002 numerator degrees of freedom (the number of schools minus one) and 20569 denominator degrees of freedom (the number of students minus the number of coefficients in the model, including the implicit coefficients for the school indicators). The p-value is well below any conventional standard, so we may conclude that there are school differences that are not fully explained by the measured predictors in the model.

School differences are also apparent in a random effects model, which I fit with PROC MIXED:

```
PROC MIXED DATA=my.nels88 COVTEST NOCLPRINT;
   CLASS schoolid;
   MODEL mathscor=sex   black hispanic asian amerind
         homework ses pared / SOLUTION;
   RANDOM INTERCEPT / SUBJECT=schoolid;
RUN;
```

In Output 2.26, the coefficients and standard errors generally fall between the fixed effects estimates and the conventional OLS estimates. The random intercept parameter has an estimated variance of 7.112, which is significantly different from 0 at below the .0001 level. This is a test of the same null hypothesis that we just tested with the F-test for the increment to R^2 in the fixed effects model, namely, that there are no school differences net of the measured predictors. But this test imposes the further restriction that the random school effect is uncorrelated with the measured predictor variables. Because of that restriction, the test has only one degree of freedom.

Output 2.26 Random Effects Analysis with PROC MIXED

		Covariance Parameter Estimates			
Cov Parm	*Subject*	*Estimate*	*Standard Error*	*Z Value*	*Pr Z*
Intercept	schoolid	7.1120	0.4884	14.56	<.0001
Residual		65.8000	0.6502	101.20	<.0001

continued

Output 2.26 *(continued)*

Effect	Estimate	Standard Error	DF	t Value	Pr > |t|
Intercept	46.9621	0.3091	1002	151.93	<.0001
sex	0.5089	0.1137	21E3	4.48	<.0001
black	-4.5306	0.2161	21E3	-20.96	<.0001
hispanic	-2.3109	0.2091	21E3	-11.05	<.0001
asian	1.7981	0.2555	21E3	7.04	<.0001
amerind	-3.7232	0.5469	21E3	-6.81	<.0001
homework	1.2244	0.04005	21E3	30.57	<.0001
ses	3.2029	0.1468	21E3	21.82	<.0001
pared	0.6919	0.08620	21E3	8.03	<.0001

Solution for Fixed Effects

In the previous section, we used PROC TSCSREG to produce a Hausman test to determine whether fixed effects coefficients were significantly different from random effects coefficients, which is equivalent to testing whether the random effect is uncorrelated with the measured predictors. Unfortunately, TSCSREG is designed for longitudinal data and can't satisfactorily accommodate the kind of structure found in the NELS data. But we can still test this hypothesis by using the group-mean centering method described in the last section. Here's the SAS code for generating the school means and deviations from the means for each variable:

```
PROC MEANS DATA=my.nels88 NWAY NOPRINT;
   CLASS schoolid;
   VAR sex black hispanic asian amerind homework ses pared;
   OUTPUT OUT=a MEAN=msex mblack mhispanic masian mamerind
          mhomework mses mpared;
RUN;
PROC SORT DATA=my.nels88;
   BY schoolid;
PROC SORT DATA=a;
   BY schoolid;
DATA combine;
   MERGE my.nels88 a;
   BY schoolid;
   dsex=sex-msex;
   dblack=black-mblack;
   dhispanic=hispanic-mhispanic;
   dasian=asian-masian;
   damerind=amerind-mamerind;
   dhomework=homework-mhomework;
   dses=ses-mses;
   dpared=pared-mpared;
RUN;
```

A random effects model is then fitted with PROC MIXED using both the means and the deviations from the means as predictors. CONTRAST statements are used to test for differences between coefficients for means and deviations, for all variables together and for each variable separately:

```
PROC MIXED DATA=combine COVTEST NOCLPRINT;
   CLASS schoolid;
   MODEL mathscor=dsex dblack dhispanic dasian damerind dhomework
         dses dpared msex mblack mhispanic masian mamerind
         mhomework mses mpared / SOLUTION;
   RANDOM INTERCEPT / SUBJECT=schoolid;
   CONTRAST 'all' dsex 1 msex -1, dblack 1 mblack -1,
            dhispanic 1 mhispanic -1, dasian 1 masian -1,
            damerind 1 mamerind -1, dhomework 1 mhomework -1,
            dses 1 mses -1, dpared 1 mpared -1;
   CONTRAST 'sex' dsex 1 msex -1;
   CONTRAST 'black' dblack 1 mblack -1;
   CONTRAST 'hispanic' dhispanic 1 mhispanic -1;
   CONTRAST 'asian' dasian 1 masian -1;
   CONTRAST 'amerind' damerind 1 mamerind -1;
   CONTRAST 'homework' dhomework 1 mhomework -1;
   CONTRAST 'ses' dses 1 mses -1;
   CONTRAST 'pared' dpared 1 mpared -1;
RUN;
```

As shown in Output 2.27, the coefficients and standard errors for the centered scores are identical to those in Output 2.24 using the fixed effects method.

Output 2.27 PROC MIXED Estimates Using Centered Scores

Covariance Parameter Estimates

Cov Parm	Subject	Estimate	Standard Error	Z Value	Pr Z
Intercept	schoolid	4.6362	0.3541	13.09	<.0001
Residual		65.6379	0.6471	101.44	<.0001

Solution for Fixed Effects

Effect	Estimate	Standard Error	DF	t Value	Pr > |t|
Intercept	40.3390	1.6123	994	25.02	<.0001
dsex	0.5139	0.1150	21E3	4.47	<.0001
dblack	-3.7572	0.2416	21E3	-15.55	<.0001
dhispanic	-1.7688	0.2274	21E3	-7.78	<.0001
dasian	1.9031	0.2640	21E3	7.21	<.0001
damerind	-2.9736	0.5662	21E3	-5.25	<.0001
dhomework	1.1816	0.04081	21E3	28.95	<.0001
dses	2.8181	0.1510	21E3	18.66	<.0001

continued

Output 2.27 *(continued)*

		Solution for Fixed Effects			
Effect	Estimate	Standard Error	DF	t Value	Pr > |t|
dpared	0.5895	0.08721	21E3	6.76	<.0001
msex	0.2632	0.6274	21E3	0.42	0.6748
mblack	-6.3276	0.4506	21E3	-14.04	<.0001
mhispanic	-3.1727	0.4928	21E3	-6.44	<.0001
masian	2.2859	0.9564	21E3	2.39	0.0169
mamerind	-9.1458	1.8784	21E3	-4.87	<.0001
mhomework	1.4761	0.1836	21E3	8.04	<.0001
mses	2.5289	0.7538	21E3	3.36	0.0008
mpared	2.7987	0.4942	21E3	5.66	<.0001

		Contrasts		
Label	Num DF	Den DF	F Value	Pr > F
all	8	21E3	46.07	<.0001
sex	1	21E3	0.15	0.6943
black	1	21E3	25.27	<.0001
hispanic	1	21E3	6.69	0.0097
asian	1	21E3	0.15	0.6996
amerind	1	21E3	9.90	0.0017
homework	1	21E3	2.45	0.1174
ses	1	21E3	0.14	0.7068
pared	1	21E3	19.38	<.0001

Results from the CONTRAST statements show that, overall, we must reject the null hypothesis that the deviation coefficients are the same as the mean coefficients. Equivalently, we must reject the hypothesis that the random school effect is uncorrelated with the measured predictor variables. But although tests for specific variables show highly significant differences for BLACK, HISPANIC, AMERIND, and PARED, the differences for SEX, ASIAN, HOMEWORK, and SES are not statistically significant, despite the large sample size. For these latter variables, it might be sensible to re-estimate the model with the constraints that the mean coefficients and deviation coefficients must be equal. This is easily accomplished by using the original rather than the centered variables:

```
PROC MIXED DATA=combine COVTEST NOCLPRINT;
   CLASS schoolid;
   MODEL mathscor=sex dblack dhispanic asian damerind homework
         ses dpared mblack mhispanic mamerind mpared / SOLUTION;
```

```
      RANDOM INTERCEPT / SUBJECT=schoolid;
   RUN;
```

The advantage of imposing these constraints is that, if they are true, we should get more efficient estimates for the coefficients. In this case, however, the differences in coefficients and their standard errors were trivial—not worth displaying.

As with the NLSY data, we can also use the centered score method to estimate hybrid models that have random slopes. For example, we can specify a model that allows the effect of parental education to vary randomly across schools by including DPARED as a variable in the RANDOM statement:

```
PROC MIXED DATA=combine COVTEST NOCLPRINT;
   CLASS schoolid;
   MODEL mathscor=dsex dblack dhispanic dasian damerind dhomework
         dses dpared msex mblack mhispanic masian mamerind
         mhomework mses mpared / SOLUTION;
   RANDOM INTERCEPT dpared / SUBJECT=schoolid;
RUN;
```

As shown in Output 2.28, parental education has a significant "average" effect on math scores (.6042), but that effect also varies randomly in magnitude across schools (as indicated by the *p*-value of .0002 for the covariance parameter for DPARED).

Output 2.28 Centered Score Model with Random Coefficient for PARED

Covariance Parameter Estimates

Cov Parm	Subject	Estimate	Standard Error	Z Value	Pr Z
Intercept	schoolid	4.6323	0.3532	13.12	<.0001
Residual		65.6361	0.6470	101.44	<.0001

Solution for Fixed Effects

Effect	Estimate	Standard Error	DF	t Value	Pr > |t|
Intercept	40.9981	0.5540	998	74.00	<.0001
sex	0.5061	0.1131	21E3	4.48	<.0001
dblack	-3.7543	0.2413	21E3	-15.56	<.0001
dhispanic	-1.7631	0.2271	21E3	-7.77	<.0001
asian	1.9307	0.2545	21E3	7.59	<.0001
damerind	-2.9672	0.5661	21E3	-5.24	<.0001
homework	1.1954	0.03984	21E3	30.01	<.0001
ses	2.8065	0.1480	21E3	18.96	<.0001
dpared	0.5929	0.08614	21E3	6.88	<.0001

continued

Output 2.28 *(continued)*

Solution for Fixed Effects

Effect	Estimate	Standard Error	DF	t Value	Pr > |t|
mblack	-6.2970	0.4199	21E3	-15.00	<.0001
mhispanic	-3.1302	0.4811	21E3	-6.51	<.0001
mamerind	-9.1411	1.8625	21E3	-4.91	<.0001
mpared	2.7345	0.1621	21E3	16.87	<.0001

2.8 Summary

Fixed effects linear models for quantitative response variables can be estimated in several different but equivalent ways:

1. If there are exactly two observations per individual, compute difference scores for all variables and then apply OLS regression to the difference scores.
2. Organize the data so that there is one record for each occasion for each individual. Do OLS with dummy variables for all individuals (less one).
3. For the data structure in method 2, express all variables as deviations from individual-level means. Then do OLS on the deviation scores, with corrections for standard errors, test statistics, and *p*-values. This is conveniently done in PROC GLM using the ABSORB statement.
4. For the data structure in method 2, express only the *predictor* variables as deviations from individual-level means. Then estimate a random effects model using PROC MIXED, with predictor variables including both the means and deviations from the means.

Of these methods, the fourth is the most flexible. It offers the following capabilities not shared with one or more of the other methods:

- the inclusion of predictor variables that do not vary within individuals
- a test of the fixed effects vs. random effects assumption
- random coefficients for those predictors that vary within individuals
- less restrictive error structures

Regardless of which computational method is used, the fixed effects method effectively controls for all individual-level covariates, both measured and unmeasured. This is its principal attraction as compared with random effects methods or GEE estimation. A key assumption of the fixed effects method, however, is that the individual-level covariates must have the same effects at all occasions. Variables whose effects are not constant across occasions must be explicitly included in the model.

Fixed Effects Methods for
Categorical Response Variables

3.1 Introduction

In this chapter we consider fixed effects regression models for response variables that are categorical: dichotomous, unordered polytomous, and ordered polytomous. In chapter 2 we saw that linear fixed effects models for quantitative response variables could be estimated in several different ways, all producing the same results. Analogous methods are also available for categorical response variables, but these methods typically do *not* produce exactly the same results. So an important task of this chapter is to clarify the differences among the different methods and to develop appropriate interpretations of their coefficients.

In chapter 1 we saw that the paired-comparisons *t*-test could be interpreted as a fixed effects method. Let's begin this chapter with an analogous method for dichotomous variables observed at two points in time. Table 3.1, taken from Hu et al. (1998), is a cross-classification of responses by sixth and seventh graders to a question about whether they had smoked cigarettes in the preceding month. They were interviewed at baseline in 1984 and again one year later.

Table 3.1 Smoking in the Preceding Month among Sixth and Seventh Graders

		One Year Later	
		Yes	No
Baseline	Yes	27	26
	No	63	566

At baseline, 8% of the respondents said they had smoked. One year later, the percentage had increased to 13. Is this change statistically significant? We can't use a conventional test for a difference between two proportions because we don't have two independent samples. McNemar's (1955) test is a simple solution to this problem. We ignore the 593 children who didn't change from baseline to one year and use only the two off-diagonal cell counts. A chi-square statistic is calculated as

$$\frac{(63-26)^2}{63+26} = 15.38$$

With 1 degree of freedom, this has a *p*-value less than .0001. We conclude that the probability of smoking increased over the one-year period.

While the hand calculation is simple enough, we can also let PROC FREQ do the work. Here's how to read in the data and get the McNemar statistic (requested with the AGREE option):

```
DATA smoking;
    INPUT baseline $ oneyear $ count;
DATALINES;
yes yes 27
yes no 26
no yes 63
no no 566
;
PROC FREQ DATA=smoking;
    WEIGHT count;
    TABLE baseline*oneyear / AGREE NOROW NOCOL NOPCT;
RUN;
```

The NOROW, NOCOL, and NOPCT options suppress the percentage calculations so that only the raw frequency counts appear in the table.

Output 3.1 PROC FREQ Output with McNemar Statistic

Table of baseline by oneyear

baseline	oneyear		
Frequency	no	yes	Total
no	566	63	629
yes	26	27	53
Total	592	90	682

continued

Output 3.1 *(continued)*

Statistics for Table of baseline by oneyear

McNemar's Test	
Statistic (S)	15.3820
DF	1
Pr > S	<.0001

The results in Output 3.1 confirm our hand calculations. Keep in mind that this test says nothing about the degree of association between the two responses. It merely tests the null hypothesis that the probability of a "yes" response is the same at the two time points, while allowing for any level of association.

Suppose we also want to answer the question "How do the odds of smoking change over the one-year period?" A natural way to answer this question is to compute the estimated odds of smoking at each interview, and then take the ratio of those odds.

$$\frac{90/592}{53/629} = 1.80$$

But a fixed effects approach leads to a different estimate, the ratio of the two off-diagonal counts: $63/26 = 2.42$. Thus a fixed effects approach leads to a much higher estimate of the change over time. The conventional method is called a *population-averaged* estimate, whereas the fixed effects estimate is called a *subject-specific* estimate. I'll have more to say about the difference between these two kinds of estimates later in this chapter. Note that this distinction was not relevant for the paired-comparisons *t*-test in the last chapter, where the difference in the means across the two time periods was the same as the mean of the differences.

While McNemar's test is well suited to its goal, it doesn't allow covariates to affect the response. In the next section we develop a logistic regression method that does just that. As we'll see, McNemar's approach can be seen as a special case of this more general method.

3.2 Logistic Models for Dichotomous Data with Two Observations Per Person

We begin with the relatively simple situation in which the response variable is a dichotomy and there are exactly two observations for each individual. As in chapter 2, we let y_{it} be the value of the response variable for individual i on occasion t, but now y is constrained to have a value of either 0 or 1. In this section, $t = 1$ or 2. Let p_{it} be the probability that $y_{it} = 1$. It is convenient to assume that the dependence of p_{it} on possible predictor variables is described by a logistic regression model

$$\log\left(\frac{p_{it}}{1 - p_{it}}\right) = \mu_t + \beta x_{it} + \gamma z_i + \alpha_i \tag{3.1}$$

where z_i is a column vector of variables that describe the individuals but do not vary over time, and x_{it} is a column vector of variables that vary both over individuals and over time for each individual. In this equation, μ_t is an intercept that is allowed to vary with time, and β and γ are row vectors of coefficients. As in chapter 2, α_i represents all differences between persons that are stable over time and not otherwise accounted for by z_i. Again, we regard these as fixed parameters, one per person. Additionally, we assume that for a given individual i (and hence a given value of α_i), y_{i1} and y_{i2} are independent. That is,

$$\Pr(y_{i1} = 0, y_{i2} = 0) = (1 - p_{i1})(1 - p_{i2})$$
$$\Pr(y_{i1} = 1, y_{i2} = 0) = p_{i1}(1 - p_{i2})$$
$$\Pr(y_{i1} = 0, y_{i2} = 1) = (1 - p_{i1})p_{i2}$$
$$\Pr(y_{i1} = 1, y_{i2} = 1) = p_{i1}p_{i2}$$

(3.2)

Our goal is to estimate μ_t and β while controlling for all time-invariant covariates (both measured and unmeasured). To accomplish that, we use only variation *within* individuals to estimate these parameters. When there are two occasions per individual, we can use a method that is very similar to the difference score method used for quantitative response variables. Let's first consider those individuals who do not change from time 1 to time 2—that is, $y_{i1} = 0$ and $y_{i2} = 0$, or $y_{i1} = 1$ and $y_{i2} = 1$. Because there is no within-individual variation on the response variable, such observations contain no information about the parameters μ and β and thus can be discarded from the analysis. That leaves individuals who change from 0 to 1 and those who change from 1 to 0. According to equations (3.2), the probability of those two outcomes is

$$\Pr(y_{i1} = 0, y_{i2} = 1) = (1 - p_{i1})p_{i2}$$

$$\Pr(y_{i1} = 1, y_{i2} = 0) = p_{i1}(1 - p_{i2})$$

We then take the logarithm of the ratio of these probabilities to get

$$\log\left(\frac{\Pr(y_{i1} = 0, y_{i2} = 1)}{\Pr(y_{i1} = 1, y_{i2} = 0)}\right) = \log(1 - p_{i1}) + \log p_{i2} - \log p_{i1} - \log(1 - p_{i2})$$

$$= \log\left(\frac{p_{i2}}{1 - p_{i2}}\right) - \log\left(\frac{p_{i1}}{1 - p_{i1}}\right)$$

Substituting from equation (3.1) and rearranging terms gives

$$\log\left(\frac{\Pr(y_{i1} = 0, y_{i2} = 1)}{\Pr(y_{i1} = 1, y_{i2} = 0)}\right) = (\mu_2 - \mu_1) + \beta(x_{i2} - x_{i1})$$

(3.3)

As we found for the linear model, both z_i and α_i have been "differenced out" of the equation. This result suggests the following method for estimating the parameters:

- Eliminate all individuals who do not change on the response variable.

- Create difference scores for all the time-varying predictors.

- Use maximum likelihood to estimate the logistic regression predicting y_{i2}, with the difference scores as predictor variables.

This procedure is called *conditional logistic regression.* I'll have more to say about its properties and justification in the next section.

If there are no covariates, we have the sort of data that we saw in Table 3.1. Here's how to estimate the logistic regression model for those tabular data:

```
PROC LOGISTIC DATA=smoking DESC;
   WHERE baseline NE oneyear;
   FREQ count;
   MODEL oneyear= / EXPB;
RUN;
```

The WHERE statement eliminates those observations that did not change from time 1 to time 2. The DESC option (short for "descending") forces PROC LOGISTIC to model the probability that the dependent variable is equal to "yes" rather than equal to "no." Although the formulas used in this chapter assume that the dependent variable y is either 1 or 0, PROC LOGISTIC can actually handle any two values, whether numeric or character. The default is to model the probability of the *lower* value, in this case lower in the alphabet. The DESC option reverses that to model the higher value. The EXPB option computes the exponentiated value of the coefficients, which can be interpreted as odds ratios.

Results in Output 3.2 are consistent with what we saw in the previous section. The odds ratio of 2.423 is just the simple ratio of the off-diagonal counts. The chi-square of 14.14 is close but not identical to the McNemar statistic of 15.38. While both statistics are testing the same null hypothesis, McNemar's test is a traditional Pearson chi-square calculated under the assumption that the two expected frequencies are the same. PROC LOGISTIC reports a Wald chi-square, which is the squared ratio of the coefficient to its estimated standard error.

Output 3.2 PROC LOGISTIC Estimates for Smoking Data

Response Profile		
Ordered Value	oneyear	Total Frequency
1	yes	63
2	no	26

continued

Output 3.2 *(continued)*

Analysis of Maximum Likelihood Estimates

Parameter	DF	Estimate	Standard Error	Wald Chi-Square	Pr > ChiSq	Exp(Est)
Intercept	1	0.8850	0.2331	14.4161	0.0001	2.423

Now let's consider an example with predictor variables. The sample consists of 1151 girls from the National Longitudinal Survey of Youth (www.bls.gov/nls) who were interviewed annually for nine years, beginning in 1979. For this example, we'll use data only from year 1 and year 5. The response variable POV has a value of 1 if the girl's household was in poverty (as defined by U.S. federal standards) in a given year, and otherwise has a value of 0. The predictor variables are:

AGE   Age in years at the first interview
BLACK   1 if respondent is black, otherwise 0
MOTHER   1 if respondent currently had a least one child, otherwise 0
SPOUSE   1 if respondent is currently living with a spouse, otherwise 0
INSCHOOL   1 if respondent is currently enrolled in school, otherwise 0
HOURS   Hours worked during the week of the survey

The first two variables are time-invariant, whereas the last four may differ at each interview.

The data set MY.TEENPOV has one record for each of the 1151 respondents, with different variable names for the same variable measured in different years. For simplicity, the data set contains only respondents who have no missing data on any of the variables. Let's first check the joint distribution of the dependent variables:

```
PROC FREQ DATA=my.teenpov;
   TABLES pov1*pov5 / NOROW NOCOL NOPCT AGREE;
RUN;
```

We see from Output 3.3 that although 445 girls changed status during the five-year period, there was only a slight increase in the proportion in poverty. This increase is not statistically significant, according to the McNemar statistic.

Output 3.3 Contingency Table for Poverty in Years 1 and 5

Table of pov1 by pov5

pov1		pov5		
Frequency		0	1	Total
	0	516	234	750
	1	211	190	401
Total		727	424	1151

continued

Output 3.3 *(continued)*

McNemar's Test	
Statistic (S)	1.1888
DF	1
Pr > S	0.2756

To do the logistic regression analysis, the first step is to create a new data set that excludes those girls whose poverty status was the same in years 1 and 5, and defines new variables that are differences between the values for year 5 and for year 1:

```
DATA teendif;
   SET my.teenpov;
   IF pov1=pov5 THEN DELETE;
   mother=mother5-mother1;
   spouse=spouse5-spouse1;
   inschool=inschool5-inschool1;
   hours=hours5-hours1;
RUN;
```

Next, we estimate a logistic regression with POV5 as the dependent variable, and difference scores and time-invariant predictors as independent variables:

```
PROC LOGISTIC DATA=teendif DESC;
   MODEL pov5=mother spouse inschool hours black age;
RUN;
```

Output 3.4 gives the results. Although the time-varying predictors are expressed as difference scores, their coefficients should be interpreted as they appear in equation (3.1)—that is, as the effect of the value of the variable in a given year on the probability of poverty in that same year. Thus, the odds ratio for MOTHER tells us that the odds of being in poverty were twice as high in years when girls had children as compared with years in which they did not have children (controlling for other variables). On the other hand, when girls lived with husbands, their odds of poverty were only 35% as large as when they did not live with husbands. Each additional hour of work per week reduced the odds of poverty by $100(1 - .967) = 3.3\%$.

Output 3.4 PROC LOGISTIC Output for Regression on Difference Scores

Response Profile		
Ordered Value	pov5	Total Frequency
1	1	234
2	0	211

continued

Output 3.4 *(continued)*

Analysis of Maximum Likelihood Estimates

Parameter	DF	Estimate	Standard Error	Wald Chi-Square	Pr > ChiSq
Intercept	1	4.8993	1.6438	8.8829	0.0029
mother	1	0.7436	0.2538	8.5862	0.0034
spouse	1	-1.0317	0.2918	12.5014	0.0004
inschool	1	0.3394	0.2178	2.4287	0.1191
hours	1	-0.0339	0.00623	29.7027	<.0001
black	1	-0.5263	0.2164	5.9154	0.0150
age	1	-0.2577	0.1029	6.2739	0.0123

Odds Ratio Estimates

Effect	Point Estimate	95% Wald Confidence Limits	
mother	2.103	1.279	3.459
spouse	0.356	0.201	0.631
inschool	1.404	0.916	2.152
hours	0.967	0.955	0.978
black	0.591	0.387	0.903
age	0.773	0.632	0.945

The coefficients (and odds ratios) for BLACK and AGE must be interpreted somewhat differently. According to equation (3.3), as time-invariant predictors these variables shouldn't even be in the model. In fact, they represent interactions between time-invariant predictor variables and time itself, so that the rate of change in the odds of poverty depends on the value of these variables. More specifically, for a girl whose predictor variables did not change from year 1 to year 5, the change in the log-odds of poverty over the five-year period can be expressed as

$$4.8993 - .5263*BLACK - .2577*AGE.$$

Thus, for a 14-year-old girl who was not black and who did not change on any of the other predictors, the predicted change in the log-odds is +1.29. Equivalently, her odds of being in poverty increase by a factor of $\exp(1.29) = 3.63$. We conclude that blacks and girls who were older at year 1 had a lower rate of increase in poverty.

As in the linear difference score model of chapter 1, we can also test for constancy in the effect of the time-varying predictors by including their values for year 1 in the model. The coefficients for the variable for year 1 represent the difference between the effects of each variable in year 1 and year 5. We see in Output 3.5 that the only time-varying predictor whose effects change significantly from year 1 to year 5 is INSCHOOL. The implied coefficient for year 5 is .6389. The implied coefficient for year 1 is .6389 − 1.1838 = −. 54449. It therefore appears that school enrollment is associated with an increased risk of poverty in the later year and a reduced risk in the earlier year. Incidentally, the proportion of girls attending school is about 89% in year 1 and 80% in year 5.

Output 3.5 Difference Regression with Variables for Year 1 Added

Analysis of Maximum Likelihood Estimates

Parameter	DF	Estimate	Standard Error	Wald Chi-Square	Pr > ChiSq
Intercept	1	3.0518	1.8261	2.7928	0.0947
mother	1	0.9093	0.2696	11.3770	0.0007
mother1	1	0.4565	0.4596	0.9868	0.3205
spouse	1	-1.0220	0.3009	11.5391	0.0007
spouse1	1	0.4422	0.7260	0.3710	0.5425
inschool	1	0.6389	0.2511	6.4722	0.0110
inschool1	1	1.1838	0.4707	6.3254	0.0119
hours	1	-0.0339	0.00677	25.0932	<.0001
hours1	1	-0.00238	0.0128	0.0343	0.8531
black	1	-0.6617	0.2264	8.5442	0.0035
age	1	-0.1961	0.1106	3.1440	0.0762

In chapter 2, we saw that the results from a difference score regression could be replicated by creating a separate record for each person at each point in time, and then estimating a regression model that includes a dummy variable for every person (except one). Let's try that for the logistic regression. The first step is to restructure the data set so there's a separate record for each person in each year:

```
DATA teenyrs2;
   SET my.teenpov;
     year=1;
     pov=pov1;
     mother=mother1;
     spouse=spouse1;
     inschool=inschool1;
     hours=hours1;
     OUTPUT;
     year=2;
     pov=pov5;
     mother=mother5;
     spouse=spouse5;
     inschool=inschool5;
     hours=hours5;
     OUTPUT;
   KEEP id year black age pov mother spouse inschool hours;
RUN;
```

The TEENYRS2 data set has 2,302 records, two for each of the 1151 girls. The time-varying covariates are given the same names for each of the two records.

Now we're ready to estimate the logistic regression model:

```
PROC LOGISTIC DATA=teenyrs2 DESC;
   CLASS id / PARAM=REF;
   MODEL pov=year mother spouse inschool hours year*black
         year*age id;
RUN;
```

The CLASS statement tells PROC LOGISTIC to create a set of dummy variables, one for each value of ID except for the highest. The PARAM=REF option says to make one of the ID numbers the reference category, by default the highest ID number. Note that in the MODEL statement, BLACK and AGE are entered as interactions with YEAR, but with no corresponding main effects.

This model took about 1.5 minutes to estimate on my PC. The printed output was extremely voluminous because LOGISTIC reported (a) a 1050 x 1050 matrix describing the coding of the dummy variables, (b) coefficients for the 1050 dummy variables, and (c) odds ratios contrasting each person with the reference person. In Output 3.6, I've excluded everything but the coefficient information from the other predictor variables.

Not only is this method cumbersome, but it also gives the wrong results. In Output 3.6, we find that every coefficient is exactly twice as large as the corresponding coefficient in Output 3.4, obtained with conditional logistic regression. This is a quite general result (Abrevaya 1997). Whenever you do logistic regression with dummy variables for individuals and exactly two observations for each individual, the coefficients will be twice as large as the coefficients from conditional logistic regression. The chi-squares and standard errors in Output 3.6 are also incorrect. The chi-squares are exactly twice as large as those in Output 3.4, and the standard errors are $\sqrt{2}$ times those in Output 3.4.

Output 3.6 Logistic Regression Estimates with Dummy Variables for Persons

				Analysis of Maximum Likelihood Estimates	
Parameter	*DF*	*Estimate*	*Standard Error*	*Wald Chi-Square*	*Pr > ChiSq*
Intercept	1	-21.3931	2293.3	0.0001	0.9926
year	1	9.7990	2.3248	17.7667	<.0001
mother	1	1.4872	0.3589	17.1744	<.0001
spouse	1	-2.0635	0.4126	25.0059	<.0001
inschool	1	0.6789	0.3080	4.8577	0.0275
hours	1	-0.0679	0.00881	59.4107	<.0001
*year*black*	1	-1.0526	0.3060	11.8321	0.0006
*year*age*	1	-0.5154	0.1455	12.5485	0.0004

When there are more than two observations per person and/or varying numbers of observations per person, there won't be such a neat scaling of the coefficients and chi-squares. In any case, logistic regression with dummy variables for individuals will generally give biased coefficient estimates. I'll have more to say about the reasons for this in the next section.

3.3 Estimation of Logistic Models for Two or More Observations Per Person

When individuals in the sample have three or more observations, we can't use the simple method of doing a logistic regression on the persons who change (with difference scores as predictors). In chapter 2, we faced the same problem with linear models, and we solved it by expressing all variables as deviations from the person-specific means. In the case of dichotomous outcomes, an analogous method can be implemented with PROC LOGISTIC (in SAS 9.0 and later).[1] Before proceeding to the practical details, I first need to clear up two theoretical issues: (1) the reason why we can't use dummy variables for individuals in logistic regression, and (2) the rationale for conditional logistic regression.

In chapter 2, we saw that one way to estimate a fixed effects linear model in the multiple observation case was to structure the data with one observation per individual per occasion and then compute an OLS regression with dummy variables for all individuals (except one). Although computationally cumbersome, that method produced the correct results. We just saw, however, that the device of using dummy variables does not work for logistic regression in the two-occasion case, and the problem extends to data with more than two occasions. The coefficients are generally biased upward, and the test statistics will also be incorrect. Why is this?

This is an example of a general problem called the *incidental parameters problem* (Kalbfleisch and Sprott 1970) that arises in certain applications of maximum likelihood estimation. The justification for maximum likelihood estimators is usually asymptotic, which means that it's based on how the estimators behave as the sample gets large. However, the validity of that justification depends on the presumption that the number of parameters remains constant as the sample gets larger. For longitudinal data, that works just fine if the number of individuals remains constant while the number of observations per individual gets larger. But if the number of individuals is getting larger while the number of time points remains constant, then the number of parameters in a fixed effects model (including coefficients of the dummy variables) is increasing at the same rate as the sample size. This is not a problem for linear models and (somewhat surprisingly) for the Poisson models discussed in chapter 4. But it is a serious problem with logistic regression and many other nonlinear regression models. The biases are greatest when, as in the previous section, the number of time points per individual is small.

The solution to the incidental parameters problem is to do *conditional maximum likelihood* (Chamberlain 1980), which we already employed in the two-occasion case. Now we need to generalize that method to more than two occasions. The basic idea is to reformulate the likelihood function so that it no longer contains the individual-specific α_i parameters in equation (3.1). It turns out that for the logistic model of equation (3.1), there are *reduced*

---

[1] Conditional logistic regression requires the STRATA statement, which was first implemented in SAS 9.0. For earlier releases, conditional logistic regression can be accomplished with PROC PHREG using the methods described in Allison (1999).

sufficient statistics for the α_i parameters. That means that there are summaries of the data that contain all the information about the α_i terms. Specifically, the reduced sufficient statistics are the counts s_i of the number of observations for each person in which $y_{it} = 1$:

$$s_i = \sum_t y_{it}$$

We can remove the α_i terms from the likelihood function by conditioning on these sufficient statistics. For a single individual, the likelihood function for conventional logistic regression is

$$\prod_t \Pr(y_{it}) = \prod_t \left(\frac{y_{it} \exp(\mu_t + \beta x_{it} + \gamma z_i + \alpha_i)}{1 + \exp(\mu_t + \beta x_{it} + \gamma z_i + \alpha_i)} \right)$$

We then condition on s_i by dividing this likelihood by the probability of observing s_i. Without going through the algebraic details, this produces

$$\frac{\prod_t \Pr(y_{it})}{\Pr(s_i)} = \frac{\psi_1}{\psi_1 + \psi_2 + \ldots + \psi_Q} \tag{3.4}$$

where

$$\psi_1 = \exp\left(\sum_t y_{it}(\mu_t + \beta x_{it}) \right)$$

In the denominator, $\psi_2, \ldots, \psi_Q$ all have the same form as ψ_1 except that, instead of the observed values of 1 and 0 for y_{it}, the 1's and 0's are permuted in all possible ways. Thus Q is the number of different ways of re-arranging the 1's and 0's, given that we've observed a certain number of each. Notice that γ, the coefficient vector for the time-invariant predictors, and the α_i terms no longer appear in this likelihood.

To put this more concretely, suppose that each person is observed on five occasions (as in our upcoming example). Suppose, further, that one particular individual was in poverty at times 1 and 3, but not at times 2, 4 or 5. We then ask the question "Given that the event occurred on two occasions, what is the probability that it happened at times 1 and 3, but not at two other times (say, 2 and 5, or 3 and 4)?" In fact, there are 10 different possible ways of choosing two occasions from among five possibilities. The resulting likelihood for this person has the following form:

$$\frac{\exp[(\mu_1 + \beta x_{i1}) + (\mu_3 + \beta x_{i3})]}{\sum_j \sum_{k>j} \exp[(\mu_j + \beta x_{ij}) + (\mu_k + \beta x_{ik})]}$$

The conditional likelihood for the whole sample is just the product of all such likelihoods for each person.

There are three things worth noting about conditional logistic regression. First, as we saw in the two-occasion case, persons who don't change on y_{it} over the period of observation are effectively eliminated from the analysis. In the likelihood (3.4), for a person who has all 1's or all 0's, the numerator and denominator will be identical and hence will cancel. With respect to the conditioning argument, if we know that someone has events on five out of five occasions, then there's no more room for variability in when those events occurred.

A second point, related to the first, is that conditional maximum likelihood estimators have two out of the three properties usually associated with maximum likelihood estimation. They are consistent (i.e., they converge in probability to the true values) and they are asymptotically normal (i.e., the sampling distribution is approximately normal for large samples). But they might not be fully efficient. There is a potential loss of information that comes from (a) excluding persons who don't change, and (b) only using within-person variation. But that's the price one always pays for choosing a fixed effects model.

A third point is that, for dichotomous dependent variables, conditional likelihood only works for the logistic regression model, not for other link functions like probit or complementary log-log. That's because those models do not have reduced sufficient statistics for the α_i parameters and thus have no way to condition them out of the likelihood function. However, for alternative link functions, it's possible to do approximate conditional likelihood using the projected score method proposed by Waterman and Lindsay (1996).

So much for the theory. How can we implement conditional logistic regression in PROC LOGISTIC? In section 3.2, we estimated a conditional logistic regression model for poverty in years 1 and 5 of a five-year series. Now let's look at all five years together. Again, the first thing we must do is restructure the data so that there is one record per person-year instead of one record per person:

```
DATA teenyrs5;
   SET my.teenpov;
   ARRAY pv(*) pov1-pov5;
   ARRAY mot(*) mother1-mother5;
   ARRAY spo(*) spouse1-spouse5;
   ARRAY ins(*) inschool1-inschool5;
   ARRAY hou(*) hours1-hours5;
   DO year=1 TO 5;
      pov=pv(year);
      mother=mot(year);
      spouse=spo(year);
      inschool=ins(year);
      hours=hou(year);
      OUTPUT;
   END;
   KEEP id year black age pov mother spouse inschool hours;
RUN;
```

This DATA step produces 5755 observations, five for each of the 1151 girls. Now we're ready to run PROC LOGISTIC to estimate the first model:

```
PROC LOGISTIC DATA=teenyrs5 DESC;
   CLASS year / PARAM=REF;
   MODEL pov = year mother spouse inschool hours;
   STRATA id;
RUN;
```

The CLASS statement declares YEAR to be a categorical variable, with the highest year (year 5) being the reference category. The STRATA statement says that each girl is a separate stratum, which groups together the five observations for each girl in the process of constructing the likelihood function.

Results in Output 3.7 are rather similar to those in Output 3.4, which was based on only two observations per person. The first panel, "Strata Summary," gives the number of girls (strata) who have specific frequencies of years in poverty. Note that there were 232 girls who were not in poverty in any of the five years and 92 girls who were in poverty all five years. Both of these groups get eliminated from the likelihood function. The second panel, "Testing Global Null Hypothesis," gives three alternative chi-square tests for the null hypothesis that all the regression coefficients are 0. Clearly that hypothesis must be rejected. Turning to the "Analysis of Maximum of Likelihood Estimates," we see that motherhood and school enrollment increase the risk of poverty, whereas living with a husband and working more hours reduce the risk. The last panel gives the odds ratios. Motherhood increases the odds of poverty by an estimated 79%. Living with a husband cuts the odds approximately in half. Each additional hour of employment per week reduces the odds by about 2%. Keep in mind that these estimates control for *all* stable characteristics of the girls, including such things as race, intelligence, place of birth, and parent's education.

Output 3.7 Conditional Logistic Regression Estimates Produced by PROC LOGISTIC

Strata Summary

Response Pattern	pov 1	pov 0	Number of Strata	Frequency
1	0	5	232	1160
2	1	4	355	1775
3	2	3	191	955
4	3	2	152	760
5	4	1	129	645
6	5	0	92	460

Testing Global Null Hypothesis: BETA=0

Test	Chi-Square	DF	Pr > ChiSq
Likelihood Ratio	97.2814	8	<.0001
Score	94.5804	8	<.0001
Wald	90.5640	8	<.0001

continued

Output 3.7 *(continued)*

Analysis of Maximum Likelihood Estimates					
Parameter	*DF*	*Estimate*	*Standard Error*	*Wald Chi-Square*	*Pr > ChiSq*
year 1	1	-0.4025	0.1275	9.9615	0.0016
year 2	1	-0.0707	0.1185	0.3562	0.5506
year 3	1	-0.0675	0.1096	0.3793	0.5380
year 4	1	0.0303	0.1047	0.0836	0.7725
mother	1	0.5824	0.1596	13.3204	0.0003
spouse	1	-0.7478	0.1753	18.1856	<.0001
inschool	1	0.2719	0.1127	5.8157	0.0159
hours	1	-0.0196	0.00315	38.8887	<.0001

Odds Ratio Estimates			
Effect	*Point Estimate*	*95% Wald Confidence Limits*	
year 1 vs 5	0.669	0.521	0.859
year 2 vs 5	0.932	0.739	1.175
year 3 vs 5	0.935	0.754	1.159
year 4 vs 5	1.031	0.840	1.265
mother	1.790	1.310	2.448
spouse	0.473	0.336	0.668
inschool	1.312	1.052	1.637
hours	0.981	0.975	0.987

Although models like this cannot include the main effects of time-invariant variables, they do allow for interactions between time-invariant variables and time-varying variables, including time itself. The next model, for example, includes the interaction between MOTHER and BLACK.

```
PROC LOGISTIC DATA=teenyrs5 DESC;
   CLASS year / PARAM=REF;
   MODEL pov = year mother spouse inschool hours mother*black;
   STRATA id;
RUN;
```

In Output 3.8, we see that the interaction is statistically significant at the .05 level. For nonblack girls, the effect of motherhood is to increase the odds[2] of poverty by a factor of

---

[2] By default, PROC LOGISTIC does not report odds ratios for variables involved in an interaction. However, these can be requested with the EXPB option on the MODEL statement.

exp(.9821) = 2.67. For black girls, on the other hand, the effect of motherhood is to increase the odds of poverty by a factor of exp(.9821 − .5989) = 1.47. Thus, motherhood has a larger effect on poverty status among nonblack girls than among black girls.

Output 3.8 Conditional Logistic Regression with Interaction

Analysis of Maximum Likelihood Estimates

Parameter		DF	Estimate	Standard Error	Wald Chi-Square	Pr > ChiSq
year	1	1	-0.3996	0.1276	9.8046	0.0017
year	2	1	-0.0677	0.1186	0.3260	0.5680
year	3	1	-0.0654	0.1097	0.3552	0.5512
year	4	1	0.0304	0.1047	0.0843	0.7716
mother		1	0.9821	0.2529	15.0787	0.0001
spouse		1	-0.7830	0.1777	19.4224	<.0001
inschool		1	0.2671	0.1128	5.6084	0.0179
hours		1	-0.0192	0.00316	36.9396	<.0001
mother*black		1	-0.5989	0.2897	4.2748	0.0387

3.4 Fixed Effects versus Random Effects

As with the linear models in chapter 2, the most popular alternative to the fixed effects model is a random effects model. That model begins with an identical equation:

$$\log\left(\frac{p_{it}}{1-p_{it}}\right) = \mu_t + \beta x_{it} + \gamma z_i + \alpha_i \tag{3.5}$$

Solving for p_{it}, this can also be written as

$$p_{it} = \frac{1}{1 + \exp(-\mu_t - \beta x_{it} - \gamma z_i - \alpha_i)} \tag{3.6}$$

Now, instead of assuming that α_i is a fixed constant, we assume that it is a random variable with the following properties:

- $E(\alpha_i) = 0$.
- $\text{Var}(\alpha_i) = \tau^2$.
- α_i is independent of x_{it} and z_i.
- α_i is normally distributed.

Models of this sort can be handled with PROC NLMIXED, which estimates a variety of nonlinear mixed models.[3] Let's apply it to our poverty example:

```
PROC NLMIXED DATA=teenyrs5;
    eta=b0 + byr1*(year=1)+ byr2*(year=2) + byr3*(year=3) +
        byr4*(year=4) + bmother*mother + bspouse*spouse +
        bschool*inschool + bhours*hours + alpha;
    p=1/(1+ EXP(-eta));
MODEL pov~BINARY(p);
RANDOM alpha ~ NORMAL(0,s2)  SUBJECT=id;
PARMS b0=-.29 byr1=-.06 byr2=.16 byr3=.09 byr4=.09
        bmother=.99 bspouse=-1.26 bschool=-.24 bhours=-.03 s2=1;
RUN;
```

The program begins by defining a linear function ETA of the explanatory variables, including a random component denoted by ALPHA. Note that each coefficient must be given a name. I've chosen names that incorporate the name of the variable so that the output is more easily interpreted. Also notice the treatment of YEAR. Since NLMIXED doesn't have a CLASS statement, I've used logical expressions like YEAR=1 to define dummy variables for the first four out of five years.

 The next statement defines the probability P of an event as a logistic function of ETA, as in equation (3.6). The MODEL statement says that the response variable POV has a Bernoulli distribution with parameter P (equivalent to a binomial distribution with $N=1$). The RANDOM statement says that there is a different random variable ALPHA for each value of the ID variable. These random variables all have normal distributions with a mean of 0 and a common variance S2. Finally, the PARMS statement sets starting values for all the parameters in the model. For the coefficients, these starting values were obtained from a simple logistic regression model estimated in PROC LOGISTIC.

Estimation of this random effects model required about 40 seconds of computer time on my PC, much longer than the fixed effects model, which ran in slightly under six seconds. Results in Output 3.9 show both similarities and differences with the fixed effects estimates in Output 3.7. The effects of motherhood and spouse are substantially larger in magnitude here than they were in Output 3.7. On the other hand, the estimate for school enrollment is much smaller and no longer statistically significant.

---

[3] As of this writing, SAS also offers an experimental procedure called GLIMMIX that might be an attractive alternative to NLMIXED. For the models discussed in this chapter, GLIMMIX has a much simpler syntax and is less computationally intensive. On the other hand, the algorithms used by GLIMMIX might be less accurate than those used by NLMIXED, especially when the number of observations per person is small.

Output 3.9 Random Effects Estimates from PROC NLMIXED

Parameter Estimates

Parameter	Estimate	Standard Error	DF	t Value	Pr > |t|	Alpha	Lower	Upper	Gradient
b0	-0.5082	0.1121	1150	-4.53	<.0001	0.05	-0.7281	-0.2883	0.000809
byr1	-0.1722	0.1152	1150	-1.49	0.1353	0.05	-0.3982	0.05385	0.000011
byr2	0.1146	0.1103	1150	1.04	0.2989	0.05	-0.1018	0.3310	-0.00045
byr3	0.05395	0.1058	1150	0.51	0.6102	0.05	-0.1536	0.2616	-0.00009
byr4	0.08755	0.1034	1150	0.85	0.3971	0.05	-0.1152	0.2903	-0.00006
bmother	1.0769	0.1185	1150	9.09	<.0001	0.05	0.8445	1.3093	-0.00006
bspouse	-1.2386	0.1521	1150	-8.14	<.0001	0.05	-1.5370	-0.9402	-0.00006
bschool	-0.06457	0.09802	1150	-0.66	0.5102	0.05	-0.2569	0.1278	0.000652
bhours	-0.02672	0.002872	1150	-9.30	<.0001	0.05	-0.03236	-0.02109	0.007776
s2	1.4490	0.1420	1150	10.20	<.0001	0.05	1.1704	1.7277	0.000012

Why the differences? Well, the important thing to keep in mind is that the random effects estimates in Output 3.9 do not control for *any* time-invariant variables, whereas the fixed effects estimates in Output 3.7 control for *all* time-invariant variables. Although time-invariant variables could be added to the random effects model, only those variables that are actually present in the data set can be statistically controlled.

3.5 Subject-Specific versus Population-Averaged Coefficients

In chapter 2, we saw that estimates for the linear random effects model could also be obtained by using GEE estimation in PROC GENMOD. Although GEE estimation also works well for logistic regression models, the results are not equivalent to the random effects estimates produced by PROC NLMIXED. Let's first examine the differences for our NLSY example, and then we'll discuss the nature of those differences. Here's a GENMOD program for a model that's similar to the one we just estimated in NLMIXED:

```
PROC GENMOD DATA=teenyrs5;
   CLASS year id;
   MODEL pov = year mother spouse inschool hours
        / DIST=BINOMIAL;
   REPEATED SUBJECT=id / TYPE=EXCH MODELSE;
RUN;
```

The DIST=BINOMIAL option specifies a binomial distribution for the response variable POV. For this distribution, the default link function is the logistic model. The REPEATED statement invokes GEE estimation (in addition to conventional maximum likelihood) for the logistic regression model. The TYPE=EXCH option says that all the within-person correlations are equal, which is similar to the random effects model. The MODELSE option requests standard errors based on the model rather than using a robust estimation method.

These two options on the REPEATED statement are not necessarily optimal but have been chosen to maximize the similarity with the random effects model. One thing that's not at all similar, however, is the computation time. While PROC NLMIXED took 40 seconds to estimate the random effects model, PROC GENMOD took only about half a second to estimate the analogous model.

Results in Output 3.10 are similar to those in Output 3.9 for the random effects model estimated by NLMIXED. The *p*-values for the coefficients are *very* close using the two methods. Although the coefficients are identical in sign and similar in magnitude, the GEE coefficients are all smaller than the random effects coefficients (except for year 3). This particular pattern is no accident. Both methods make similar assumptions about the data, but the random effects maximum likelihood method produces *subject-specific coefficients* whereas the GEE method produces *population-averaged coefficients* (Hu et al. 1998; Diggle et al. 1994, Ch. 7).

Output 3.10 GEE Estimates from PROC GENMOD

Analysis Of GEE Parameter Estimates							
Model-Based Standard Error Estimates							
Parameter		*Estimate*	*Standard Error*	*95% Confidence Limits*		*Z*	*Pr > |Z|*
Intercept		0.4019	0.0868	0.2317	0.5721	4.63	<.0001
year	1	0.1331	0.0892	-0.0418	0.3080	1.49	0.1358
year	2	-0.0915	0.0854	-0.2589	0.0759	-1.07	0.2840
year	3	-0.0435	0.0820	-0.2041	0.1172	-0.53	0.5958
year	4	-0.0713	0.0800	-0.2281	0.0855	-0.89	0.3728
year	5	0.0000	0.0000	0.0000	0.0000	.	.
mother		-0.8450	0.0919	-1.0251	-0.6650	-9.20	<.0001
spouse		0.9847	0.1206	0.7484	1.2211	8.16	<.0001
inschool		0.0471	0.0763	-0.1024	0.1966	0.62	0.5373
hours		0.0216	0.0023	0.0171	0.0260	9.41	<.0001
Scale		1.0000	.	.	.	.	.

What's the difference? A subject-specific coefficient is an estimate of what would happen to a particular individual if the predictor variable were increased by one unit. A population-averaged coefficient, on the other hand, is an estimate of what would happen to the whole population if everyone's predictor variable were raised by one unit. For linear models, there is no difference. But for logistic regression models, and for many other nonlinear models, subject-specific coefficients will typically be larger than population-averaged coefficients.

Which is preferable? Well, that depends. Suppose you're a doctor and you want to know how much a flu vaccine will lower your patient's risk of getting infected. Then the subject-specific coefficient is what you want. On the other hand, if you're a public-health administrator and you want to know how the proportion of people who contract some disease will change if everyone is vaccinated, then the population-averaged coefficient might be more useful. But even in the latter case, there's a sense in which the subject-specific coefficient is more fundamental.

Suppose that the true model is the basic random effects logistic model of equation (3.5). The coefficient vectors β and γ are both subject specific. But if we estimate the model with GEE using PROC GENMOD, we will get population-averaged coefficients β^* and γ^*. The degree to which these coefficients differ depends on the variance of α_i. Specifically, if $\text{Var}(\alpha_i) = 0$, then $\beta = \beta^*$ and $\gamma = \gamma^*$. As $\text{Var}(\alpha_i)$ increases, the values of β^* and γ^* decline toward 0. When α_i has a normal distribution, the approximate relationship is

$$\beta^* \approx \frac{\beta}{\sqrt{.346\,\text{var}(\alpha_i) + 1}}$$

So the population-averaged coefficients depend on the degree of unobserved heterogeneity in the logistic regression model. Comparing Outputs 3.9 and 3.10, we find that this relationship does, in fact, hold approximately.

If your main concern is with the statistical significance and relative importance of the variables in the model, the population-averaged results obtained with GEE estimation may be quite adequate. Given the computational economy of GENMOD, that may be the way to go. But if you really want to get the best estimate of the magnitudes of the subject-specific effects, the coefficients produced by NLMIXED are preferable. Note, also, that coefficients for the fixed effects logistic regression model, as estimated by conditional logistic regression using LOGISTIC, are also subject-specific and thus are not deflated by unobserved heterogeneity.

3.6 A Hybrid Model

In chapter 2, we saw how linear models with fixed and random effects could be combined into a single model by decomposing the time-varying predictors into within-person and between-person components, and by including both components in a random effects model. We can do the same for the logistic regression model, but, unfortunately, things don't work out quite so neatly.

As before, the first step is to calculate person-specific means and deviations from those means for the time-varying predictors:

```
PROC SORT DATA=teenyrs5;
   BY id;
PROC MEANS DATA=teenyrs5 NWAY NOPRINT;
   CLASS id;
   VAR  mother spouse inschool hours;
   OUTPUT OUT=means MEAN=mmother mspouse mschool mhours;
RUN;
```

The CLASS statement tells PROC MEANS to calculate the means separately for each value of the ID variable. The OUTPUT statement says to write the means onto a new data set MEANS, with one record for each person. Next, we merge the means with the original data set and calculate deviation scores:

```
DATA teencomb;
   MERGE teenyrs5 means;
   BY id;
   dmother=mother-mmother;
   dspouse=spouse-mspouse;
   dschool=inschool-mschool;
   dhours=hours-mhours;
RUN;
```

Using PROC NLMIXED, the next step is to run a random effects model with both the person-specific means and the deviations from those means, along with year effects and effects of time-invariant variables (BLACK and AGE in this analysis):

```
PROC NLMIXED DATA=teencomb;
   eta=b0 + byr1*(year=1)+ byr2*(year=2) + byr3*(year=3) +
      byr4*(year=4) + bdmother*dmother + bdspouse*dspouse +
      bdschool*dschool + bdhours*dhours + bmmother*mmother +
      bmspouse*mspouse + bmschool*mschool + bmhours*mhours +
      bblack*black +bage*age + alpha;
   p=1/(1+ EXP(-eta));
MODEL pov~BINARY(p);
RANDOM alpha ~ NORMAL(0,s2)  SUBJECT=id;
PARMS b0=1.9 byr1=-.3 byr2=-.04 byr3=-.05 byr4=.03 bdmother=.5
      bdspouse=-.7 bdschool=.2 bdhours=-.02 bmmother=.9
      bmspouse=-1.7 bmschool=-1 bmhours=-.04 bblack=.5 bage=-.1
      s2=1;
CONTRAST 'Test of fixed vs. random' bdmother-bmmother, bdspouse-
         bmspouse, bdschool-bmschool, bdhours-bmhours;
RUN;
```

A CONTRAST statement is included to test whether the coefficients for the deviation variables are the same as the coefficients for the corresponding mean variables. The text in quotes is just a user-chosen label for the output. The null hypothesis being tested is that all the parameter differences, separated by commas, are equal to 0. In effect, this is a test of the random effects versus fixed effects approach.

Results are shown in Output 3.11. We see that the coefficients, standard errors, and p-values for the deviation variables are very close to those we got with conditional logistic regression in Output 3.7. They are not identical, however, in contrast to what we found for linear models in chapter 2. For example, the conditional logistic regression estimate for the effect of SPOUSE was $-.748$ with a standard error .175. Here, the estimate is $-.817$ with a standard error of .179. So it seems that that the hybrid method does not exactly reproduce the fixed effects estimates obtained with conditional logistic regression.

Output 3.11 Hybrid Model Estimates Produced by PROC NLMIXED

Parameter Estimates

Parameter	Estimate	Standard Error	DF	t Value	Pr > |t|	Alpha	Lower	Upper	Gradient
b0	1.9350	0.8170	1150	2.37	0.0180	0.05	0.3320	3.5381	-0.54682
byr1	-0.3899	0.1251	1150	-3.12	0.0019	0.05	-0.6353	-0.1444	-0.17353
byr2	-0.05712	0.1167	1150	-0.49	0.6247	0.05	-0.2862	0.1719	-0.08998
byr3	-0.06143	0.1084	1150	-0.57	0.5710	0.05	-0.2741	0.1512	-0.27951
byr4	0.04193	0.1036	1150	0.40	0.6858	0.05	-0.1614	0.2452	0.248893
bdmother	0.5960	0.1582	1150	3.77	0.0002	0.05	0.2855	0.9064	0.066562
bdspouse	-0.8168	0.1795	1150	-4.55	<.0001	0.05	-1.1689	-0.4647	-0.31346
bdschool	0.2726	0.1128	1150	2.42	0.0158	0.05	0.05126	0.4940	-0.14887
bdhours	-0.02102	0.003207	1150	-6.56	<.0001	0.05	-0.02731	-0.01473	-1.79542
bmmother	1.0801	0.1801	1150	6.00	<.0001	0.05	0.7267	1.4336	-0.04581
bmspouse	-2.1409	0.2546	1150	-8.41	<.0001	0.05	-2.6405	-1.6413	0.045393
bmschool	-1.3305	0.2013	1150	-6.61	<.0001	0.05	-1.7254	-0.9356	-0.23929
bmhours	-0.04705	0.005817	1150	-8.09	<.0001	0.05	-0.05846	-0.03564	1.025076
bblack	0.5653	0.09673	1150	5.84	<.0001	0.05	0.3755	0.7551	-0.73213
bage	-0.1020	0.04971	1150	-2.05	0.0404	0.05	-0.1995	-0.00446	0.045949
s2	1.2366	0.1268	1150	9.75	<.0001	0.05	0.9879	1.4854	-0.3998

Contrasts

Label	Num DF	Den DF	F Value	Pr > F
Test of fixed vs. random	4	1150	19.34	<.0001

There are two important advantages to the hybrid method. First, it allows one to get coefficient estimates for the time-invariant covariates. We see here, for example, that blacks have significantly higher rates of poverty, while girls who were older at the first interview have significantly lower rates of poverty. Keep in mind that these estimates do not control for unobserved, stable covariates. Second, the hybrid method allows for a test of the random effects model (the null hypothesis) versus the less restrictive fixed effects model. From the results of the CONTRAST statement in Output 3.11, we see that the random effects model must be rejected in favor of the fixed effects model.

These advantages come with a substantial computational cost. While PROC LOGISTIC took about five seconds to estimate the conditional logistic regression, PROC NLMIXED took four *minutes* to estimate the hybrid model. Clearly, this could be prohibitive with a very large sample (or a slow computer). There is an alternative, however. Instead of doing maximum likelihood estimation of the random effects model with NLMIXED, we can do GEE estimation of an equivalent model using PROC GENMOD. Here's how to set it up:

```
PROC GENMOD DATA=teencomb DESC;
   CLASS id year;
   MODEL pov = year dmother dspouse dschool dhours mmother
         mspouse mschool mhours black age / DIST=BINOMIAL;
   CONTRAST 'Test of fixed vs. random' dmother 1 mmother -1,
            dspouse 1 mspouse -1,dschool 1 mschool -1,
            dhours 1 / mhours -1;
   REPEATED SUBJECT=id / TYPE=EXCH MODELSE;
RUN;
```

The CONTRAST statement in PROC GENMOD has a very different syntax than what we just saw for PROC NLMIXED. It's essentially the same syntax that we used for PROC MIXED in chapter 2. The TYPE=EXCH and MODELSE options are used here to maximize the similarity with PROC NLMIXED. In practice, the estimates might be more robust with TYPE=UN (for unstructured correlation matrix) and the empirical standard errors (which are the default). In contrast to NLMIXED, estimation with GENMOD required less than three seconds of computing time.

Results are shown in Output 3.12. Comparing the GENMOD *p*-values with the NLMIXED *p*-values in Output 3.11, we find that they are very close in every case. While the GENMOD coefficients are identical in sign to the NLMIXED coefficients, they are always a bit smaller in magnitude. That's consistent with the earlier point that GEE estimation produces population-averaged coefficients, which are usually closer to zero than the subject-specific coefficients produced by maximum likelihood estimation of a random effects model. In any case, it does appear that GENMOD is a good alternative for estimating the hybrid model in those cases where NLMIXED would be computationally impractical.

Output 3.12 Hybrid Estimates Produced by PROC GENMOD

Analysis Of GEE Parameter Estimates

Model-Based Standard Error Estimates

Parameter		Estimate	Standard Error	95% Confidence Limits		Z	Pr > |Z|
Intercept		-1.9204	0.6680	-3.2296	-0.6112	-2.87	0.0040
year	1	0.3144	0.1014	0.1156	0.5132	3.10	0.0019
year	2	0.0449	0.0947	-0.1407	0.2305	0.47	0.6356
year	3	0.0483	0.0880	-0.1241	0.2207	0.55	0.5830
year	4	-0.0338	0.0842	-0.1989	0.1313	-0.40	0.6881
year	5	0.0000	0.0000	0.0000	0.0000	.	.
dmother		-0.4838	0.1284	-0.7355	-0.2322	-3.77	0.0002
dspouse		0.6733	0.1483	0.3826	0.9640	4.54	<.0001
dschool		-0.2248	0.0922	-0.4055	-0.0442	-2.44	0.0147
dhours		0.0175	0.0026	0.0123	0.0226	6.61	<.0001
mmother		-0.8759	0.1452	-1.1604	-0.5914	-6.03	<.0001
mspouse		1.7709	0.2106	1.3582	2.1836	8.41	<.0001

continued

Output 3.12 *(continued)*

Analysis Of GEE Parameter Estimates

Model-Based Standard Error Estimates

Parameter	Estimate	Standard Error	95% Confidence Limits		Z	Pr > |Z|
mschool	1.1220	0.1644	0.7998	1.4443	6.82	<.0001
mhours	0.0402	0.0048	0.0307	0.0497	8.30	<.0001
black	-0.4757	0.0785	-0.6295	-0.3218	-6.06	<.0001
AGE	0.1032	0.0406	0.0237	0.1828	2.54	0.0110
Scale	1.0000	.	.	.	.	.

Contrast Results for GEE Analysis

Contrast	DF	Chi-Square	Pr > ChiSq	Type
test of fixed vs. random	4	79.99	<.0001	Score

3.7 Fixed Effects Methods for Multinomial Responses

So far, this chapter has dealt only with binary response variables. We now consider a categorical response variable y_{it} that can take on more than two values. Without loss of generality, let's suppose that those values are the integers ranging from 1 to J. Let $p_{ijt} = \text{Prob}(y_{it} = j)$. We now want a model for the dependence of this probability on predictors x_{it} and z_i.

We begin with the simpler case in which we assume an ordering of the J categories. The most popular model for ordered categorical data is the *cumulative logit model* which, in its conventional form, is available in both PROC LOGISTIC and PROC GENMOD. A fixed effects version of the model can be written as

$$\log\left(\frac{F_{ijt}}{1-F_{ijt}}\right) = \mu_{tj} + \beta x_{it} + \gamma z_i + \alpha_i \qquad j = 1,...,J-1$$

where $F_{ijt} = \sum_{m=j}^{J} p_{imt}$ is the "cumulative" probability of being in category j or higher.

Unfortunately, this model does not have reduced sufficient statistics for the α_i parameters. Thus, conditional maximum likelihood is not an option for estimation. One approach to estimation would be the approximate conditional method proposed by Waterman and Lindsay (1996), but that's not available in any commercial software. However, we *can* apply the hybrid method discussed in the previous section using robust standard errors to adjust for the lack of independence in the repeated observations for each individual.

As an example, we'll analyze data on a sample of 396 people who survived residential fires in the Philadelphia area (Keane et al. 1996). They were interviewed at 3 months, 6 months, and 12 months after the fire. The outcome variable FORGIVE is a response to the question "Have you had feelings that it is difficult to forgive yourself for anything that happened during the fire?" The possible responses were coded as follows:

1   Not at all

2   A little

3   Somewhat

4   Very much

The working data set contains 1,188 records, three for each person, corresponding to the three interviews. The predictor variables, measured at each interview, are

DEPRESS   A depression scale with values ranging from 1 to 4

RELSER   A measure of attendance at religious services: 1=never, 2=occasional, 3=regular

SEVENT   Number of stressful events that have occurred since the fire or since the last interview, ranging from 0 to 5

There is also a variable SUBJID which is the id number for each person and is common to all three records for each person.

To implement the hybrid method, we must calculate person-specific means for each of the variables, merge those into the original data set, and then calculate deviations from those means:

```
PROC MEANS DATA=my.forgive NWAY NOPRINT;
   CLASS subjid;
   VAR relser control depress  sevent ;
   OUTPUT OUT=means MEAN= mrelser mcontrol mdepress  msevent;
RUN;
DATA forgive;
   MERGE my.forgive means;
   BY subjid;
   dcontrol=control-mcontrol;
   ddepress=depress-mdepress;
   drelser=relser-mrelser;
   dsevent=sevent-msevent;
RUN;
```

Now we're ready to estimate the cumulative logit model with PROC GENMOD:

```
PROC GENMOD DATA=forgive;
   CLASS time subjid;
   MODEL forgive=  ddepress drelser dsevent
         mdepress mrelser msevent time / D=MULTINOMIAL;
   REPEATED SUBJECT=subjid / TYPE=IND;
   CONTRAST 'Fixed vs. Random Effects' ddepress 1 mdepress -1,
            drelser 1 mrelser -1, dsevent 1 msevent -1;
RUN;
```

The D=MULTINOMIAL option specifies that the dependent variable FORGIVE has a multinomial distribution with a cumulative link to the predictor variables. The default is a cumulative *logit* link (as opposed to probit or complementary log-log). Note that because I did not put the DESC option on the PROC statement, this model predicts the probability of the response variable having a lower value (less likelihood of difficulty forgiving oneself).

The REPEATED statement invokes GEE estimation, with standard errors and associated statistics calculated using the robust method of White (1980). Note that TYPE=IND is the only correlation structure allowed whenever D=MULTINOMIAL is specified. This means that GEE estimation presumes that there is no correlation among the repeated measures, and implies that GEE coefficient estimates are identical to those produced by conventional maximum likelihood. Nevertheless, the standard errors and test statistics *are* adjusted for dependence among the observations. Finally, the CONTRAST statement tests whether the coefficients for the deviation variables are the same as the coefficients for the corresponding mean variables. As we've seen before, this is equivalent to testing for fixed effects versus random effects.

Output 3.13 Hybrid Estimates for Cumulative Logit Model with PROC GENMOD

Analysis Of GEE Parameter Estimates

Empirical Standard Error Estimates

Parameter		Estimate	Standard Error	95% Confidence Limits		Z	Pr > |Z|
Intercept1		-3.7853	0.3653	-4.5012	-3.0693	-10.36	<.0001
Intercept2		-2.9643	0.3492	-3.6487	-2.2799	-8.49	<.0001
Intercept3		-2.1085	0.3422	-2.7791	-1.4378	-6.16	<.0001
ddepress		0.3001	0.1389	0.0278	0.5724	2.16	0.0308
drelser		0.1462	0.1600	-0.1673	0.4598	0.91	0.3606
dsevent		0.1728	0.0798	0.0165	0.3292	2.17	0.0303
mdepress		0.7831	0.1258	0.5365	1.0298	6.22	<.0001
mrelser		-0.3619	0.1572	-0.6700	-0.0538	-2.30	0.0213
msevent		0.0579	0.1294	-0.1957	0.3116	0.45	0.6543
time	1	0.7816	0.1712	0.4460	1.1172	4.56	<.0001
time	2	0.4850	0.1696	0.1526	0.8175	2.86	0.0042
time	3	0.0000	0.0000	0.0000	0.0000	.	.

Contrast Results for GEE Analysis

Contrast	DF	Chi-Square	Pr > ChiSq	Type
Fixed vs. Random Effects	3	11.87	0.0078	Score

Results are displayed in Output 3.13. The coefficients for the three deviation variables (those whose names begin with D) can be interpreted as if they were fixed effects coefficients. Because these coefficients depend only on variation over time within persons, they control for all stable covariates. Among these coefficients, we see significant effects of depression and number of stressful events. As expected, those who are more depressed and who had more stressful events are more likely to have trouble forgiving themselves. It's clear, on the other hand, that the deviation score for attendance at religious services does *not* have an effect, even though the mean score is significant at the .02 level. The results from the CONTRAST statement indicate that we should reject the null hypothesis that the deviation coefficients are the same as the corresponding mean coefficients. The implication is that we should focus our attention on the deviation coefficients, since they control for all stable covariates.

As we have previously observed, one limitation of the GEE method is that the coefficients are population averaged rather than subject specific, implying that they are attenuated toward zero because of population heterogeneity. If you're willing to put in some additional programming effort and computer time, you can avoid this problem by fitting a random effects model with PROC NLMIXED. Because the cumulative logit model is not built into NLMIXED, however, the programming is somewhat more involved:

```
PROC NLMIXED DATA=forgive;
   eta=bddepress*ddepress + bdrelser*drelser + bdsevent*dsevent
       + bmdepress*mdepress + bmrelser*mrelser + bmsevent*msevent +
         t1*(time EQ 1) + t2*(time EQ 2) + alpha;
   IF forgive=1 THEN p=1/(1+EXP(-b1-eta));
   ELSE IF forgive=2 THEN p=1/(1+EXP(-b2-eta))-1/(1+EXP(-b1-
         eta));
   ELSE IF forgive=3 THEN p=1/(1+EXP(-b3-eta))-1/(1+EXP(-b2-
         eta));
   ELSE p=1-1/(1+EXP(-b3-eta));
   ll=LOG(p);
   MODEL forgive~GENERAL(ll);
   RANDOM alpha~NORMAL(0,var) SUBJECT=subjid;
   CONTRAST 'Test of fixed vs. random' bddepress-bmdepress,
            bdrelser-bmrelser,bdsevent-bmsevent,bdsevent-
            bmsevent;
   PARMS  bddepress=0 bdrelser=0 bdsevent=0 bmdepress=0
          bmrelser=0 bmsevent=0 t1=0 t2=0 b1=1 b2=2 b3=3 var=1;
RUN;
```

The first statement after the PROC statement defines ETA to be a linear function of the explanatory variables, including a random disturbance term ALPHA. As with previous NLMIXED programs, I've chosen names for the coefficients that are the same as the names for the covariates, except prefixed by B, making it easier to interpret the output. The next four IF and ELSE IF statements specify the probability P of observing each outcome of the response variable, as it depends on ETA. The log-likelihood LL is defined to equal the log of the probability P. The MODEL statement says simply that the response variable FORGIVE has a log-likelihood given by LL. The RANDOM statement declares ALPHA to be normally distributed with a mean of 0 and a variance parameter VAR. The CONTRAST statement tests whether the coefficients for the deviation variables are the same as the coefficients for the corresponding mean variables. Finally, the PARMS statement assigns starting values to all the parameters.

The coefficient estimates in Output 3.14 generally follow the same pattern as those in Output 3.13 produced by PROC GENMOD, but their magnitudes are all noticeably larger. This is just what we would expect from a subject-specific method. The increased magnitude does not always imply an increased level of statistical significance, however, because the standard errors also increase. For example, the coefficient for DSEVENT has a *p*-value of .03 in Output 3.13 and .09 in Output 3.14. Another thing to keep in mind is that PROC GENMOD took 0.2 seconds to estimate the model on my PC, whereas PROC NLMIXED took 8 seconds.

Output 3.14 Estimates for Cumulative Logit Model with PROC NLMIXED

Parameter Estimates

Parameter	Estimate	Standard Error	DF	t Value	Pr > |t|	Alpha	Lower	Upper	Gradient
bddepress	-0.5128	0.1948	395	-2.63	0.0088	0.05	-0.8957	-0.1298	0.000115
bdrelser	-0.2621	0.2324	395	-1.13	0.2602	0.05	-0.7191	0.1949	-0.00007
bdsevent	-0.2319	0.1380	395	-1.68	0.0935	0.05	-0.5032	0.03927	0.000148
bmdepress	-1.2357	0.2041	395	-6.05	<.0001	0.05	-1.6369	-0.8344	-0.00013
bmrelser	0.6043	0.2408	395	2.51	0.0125	0.05	0.1310	1.0777	-0.00004
bmsevent	-0.09638	0.2235	395	-0.43	0.6665	0.05	-0.5357	0.3430	-0.00006
t1	-1.1166	0.2639	395	-4.23	<.0001	0.05	-1.6355	-0.5978	0.000016
t2	-0.6750	0.2521	395	-2.68	0.0077	0.05	-1.1706	-0.1794	0.000035
b1	3.2332	0.5851	395	5.53	<.0001	0.05	2.0829	4.3835	-0.00004
b2	4.5390	0.6096	395	7.45	<.0001	0.05	3.3406	5.7374	-0.00004
b3	5.6948	0.6374	395	8.93	<.0001	0.05	4.4416	6.9480	0.00005
var	4.1569	0.8213	395	5.06	<.0001	0.05	2.5422	5.7716	-4.26E-6

Contrasts

Label	Num DF	Den DF	F Value	Pr > F
Test of fixed vs. random	3	395	4.60	0.0035

Now let's consider the more complicated situation in which the *J* categories are unordered. The most popular model for unordered dependent variables is the multinomial logit model (also known as the generalized logit model), which we now extend to include fixed effects:

$$\log\left(\frac{p_{ij}}{p_{iJ}}\right) = \mu_{jt} + \beta_j x_{it} + \gamma_j z_i + \alpha_{ij}, \quad j = 1,\ldots,J-1$$

In essence, this is a set of binary logistic regression equations that simultaneously compare each category to the last category. Notice that the fixed effects α_{ij} vary both over individuals and over response values.

As with a single binary logistic model (a special case of the multinomial model), there are reduced sufficient statistics for the α_{ij} terms, namely the frequency counts over time of the different response values for each individual. By conditioning on those counts, this model can be estimated by conditional maximum likelihood. Unfortunately, there are no SAS procedures that are designed to do this. For certain simple cases in which the time-varying covariates are categorical, the model can be reformulated as a log-linear model that can be estimated with PROC GENMOD or PROC CATMOD (Tjur 1982; Conaway 1989; Darroch and McCloud 1986; Kenward and Jones 1991), but I will not pursue those methods here. Alternatively, one could break the multinomial model into a set of binary models, one model for each comparison of a particular category with a reference category (Begg and Gray 1984; Allison 1999). Each binary model could then be estimated using the conditional logistic regression methods we have already discussed in this chapter. While this approach produces consistent estimates (in the statistical sense) of the coefficients, results will differ depending on the choice of the reference category. Furthermore, there is no overall test for the effect of each variable on the response variable.

As with the cumulative logit model, it seems that the best available approach in SAS is to use the hybrid method. In fact, we can use the same data set that we created earlier for estimating the cumulative model. Unfortunately, PROC GENMOD will not estimate an unordered multinomial model, and PROC LOGISTIC does not allow for dependence among the repeated observations. Instead, we shall use PROC SURVEYLOGISTIC, which does conventional maximum likelihood estimation of the coefficients but produces standard errors and test statistics that allow for dependence among the repeated observations. Here's the code:

```
PROC SURVEYLOGISTIC DATA=forgive;
   CLASS time;
   MODEL forgive(REF='1')=  ddepress drelser dsevent
          mdepress mrelser msevent time / LINK=GLOGIT;
   CLUSTER subjid;
   CONTRAST 'Fixed vs. Random Effects' ddepress 1 mdepress -1,
            drelser 1 mrelser -1, dsevent 1 msevent -1;
RUN;
```

The syntax of PROC SURVEYLOGISTIC is nearly identical to that of PROC LOGISTIC except, in this example, for the CLUSTER statement. The CLUSTER statement specifies an id variable that defines groups within which observations are allowed to be dependent. In the MODEL statement, the REF= '1' option specifies that the reference category for the dependent variable will be 1, which is the value for 83% of the cases. The default is to choose the highest value (in this case 5) as the reference category, but only about 4% of the cases have that value. Although the generalized logit model is fundamentally invariant to the choice of the reference category, choosing a reference category with few cases can make it appear as though none of the coefficients is statistically significant.

The LINK=GLOGIT option tells SAS that this is a generalized (unordered) logit model rather than the cumulative logit model, which is the default. The CONTRAST statement tests the null hypothesis that all the deviation coefficients are identical to all the corresponding mean coefficients. Although the syntax is the same as the CONTRAST statement for the cumulative model in GENMOD, the consequences are somewhat different. In our unordered model, each predictor variable has three coefficients. Each coefficient measures the effect of the variable on being in one particular category rather than the reference category. When the CONTRAST statement specifies, say, DDEPRESS 1 MDEPRESS –1, each of the three coefficients for DDEPRESS is compared with the corresponding coefficients for MDEPRESS. Thus, the chi-square statistic produced by our CONTRAST statement has nine degrees of freedom (three variables × three coefficients).

Results are shown in Output 3.15. The "Type 3 Analysis of Effects" panel gives chi-squares for the null hypotheses that all three coefficients for each variable are zero, controlling for all the other variables. These chi-squares are invariant to the choice of the reference category. We see that none of the fixed effects deviation variables is statistically significant.

The "Analysis of Maximum Likelihood Estimates" panel reports the individual coefficient estimates and associated statistics. As already noted, these coefficients are conventional maximum likelihood estimates under the assumption that all observations are independent. Hence, they are the same numbers that would be produced by PROC LOGISTIC with the LINK=GLOGIT option. The standard errors, on the other hand, are adjusted for dependence among the repeated observations for each person. In fact, they are not all that different from the standard errors produced by PROC LOGISTIC (or PROC SURVEYLOGISTIC without the CLUSTER statement). Finally, the results for the CONTRAST statement provide marginal evidence that the deviation coefficients are different from the mean coefficients.

Output 3.15 Estimates for Generalized Logit Model with PROC SURVEYLOGISTIC

Type 3 Analysis of Effects

Effect	DF	Wald Chi-Square	Pr > ChiSq
ddepress	3	6.0613	0.1087
drelser	3	1.4103	0.7031
dsevent	3	5.5606	0.1351
mdepress	3	37.0442	<.0001
mrelser	3	7.3868	0.0605
msevent	3	0.9435	0.8149
time	6	24.4000	0.0004

Analysis of Maximum Likelihood Estimates

Parameter	forgive	DF	Estimate	Standard Error	Wald Chi-Square	Pr > ChiSq
Intercept	2	1	-2.0965	0.3992	27.5840	<.0001
Intercept	3	1	-3.3333	0.5462	37.2401	<.0001
Intercept	4	1	-3.4458	0.5699	36.5541	<.0001
ddepress	2	1	0.2869	0.2154	1.7746	0.1828
ddepress	3	1	0.0597	0.2625	0.0518	0.8200
ddepress	4	1	0.5162	0.2418	4.5566	0.0328
drelser	2	1	0.0979	0.2933	0.1114	0.7386
drelser	3	1	0.1264	0.4082	0.0958	0.7569
drelser	4	1	0.3057	0.3016	1.0275	0.3107

continued

Output 3.15 *(continued)*

Analysis of Maximum Likelihood Estimates

Parameter	forgive		DF	Estimate	Standard Error	Wald Chi-Square	Pr > ChiSq
dsevent	2		1	0.1197	0.1450	0.6820	0.4089
dsevent	3		1	0.0869	0.1907	0.2076	0.6487
dsevent	4		1	0.2961	0.1505	3.8730	0.0491
mdepress	2		1	0.6285	0.1362	21.3044	<.0001
mdepress	3		1	0.8142	0.1783	20.8480	<.0001
mdepress	4		1	1.0347	0.2091	24.4928	<.0001
mrelser	2		1	-0.4500	0.1715	6.8824	0.0087
mrelser	3		1	-0.2040	0.2703	0.5694	0.4505
mrelser	4		1	-0.3816	0.2572	2.2015	0.1379
msevent	2		1	0.1280	0.1404	0.8313	0.3619
msevent	3		1	-0.00520	0.2073	0.0006	0.9800
msevent	4		1	0.0326	0.2266	0.0207	0.8856
time	1	2	1	0.1745	0.1571	1.2343	0.2666
time	1	3	1	0.5163	0.1682	9.4245	0.0021
time	1	4	1	0.5069	0.1911	7.0390	0.0080
time	2	2	1	0.1984	0.1404	1.9957	0.1577
mdepress	4		1	1.0347	0.2091	24.4928	<.0001
mrelser	2		1	-0.4500	0.1715	6.8824	0.0087

Contrast Test Results

Contrast	DF	Wald Chi-Square	Pr > ChiSq
Fixed vs. Random Effects	9	16.0781	0.0653

3.8 Summary

In this chapter we've seen how the fixed effects methods developed for continuous response variables in chapter 2 can be extended to categorical response variables. Most of the chapter focused on regression models for dichotomous responses. When there are just two dichotomous observations for each individual, a fixed effects regression model can be estimated by (a) discarding all cases that have the same values on the two response variables, (b) recoding all time-varying explanatory variables as difference scores, and (c) fitting a conventional logistic regression model to one of the response variables. This is a form of conditional maximum likelihood.

We then considered the more general case where individuals may have more than two dichotomous response observations. As in chapter 2, the first step is to reorganize the data so that there is a separate record for each response for each individual. But unlike the linear models in chapter 2, it is not legitimate to estimate a conventional logistic regression model with dummy variables for the individuals. Because of the *incidental parameters problem*, the coefficients from such a regression will be upwardly biased. Instead, we use conditional maximum likelihood to "condition out" the fixed effects. In SAS, this is accomplished with the STRATA statement in PROC LOGISTIC.

Possible alternatives to fixed effects logistic regression are GEE estimation of logistic regression models with PROC GENMOD and random effects logistic regression models estimated with PROC NLMIXED. Unlike the fixed effects approach, neither of these methods controls for unmeasured, time-invariant explanatory variables. Among these two methods, PROC NLMIXED has the advantage of producing *subject-specific* rather than *population-averaged* coefficients. Population-averaged coefficients are generally attenuated toward zero by unobserved heterogeneity. We then combined the fixed effects and random effects approaches into a hybrid model by decomposing time-varying covariates into individual mean values and deviations from those means. This can be accomplished with either PROC GENMOD or PROC NLMIXED.

Finally, we considered how these approaches might be extended to response variables with more than two categories. Although conditional maximum likelihood could, in principle, be applied to unordered, multinomial response models, there is currently no SAS procedure that will accomplish this in general cases. For ordered multinomial responses, a hybrid cumulative logit model can be estimated with GENMOD or NLMIXED. For unordered multinomial responses, a hybrid generalized logit model can be estimated with PROC SURVEYLOGISTIC.

Fixed Effects Regression Methods for Count Data

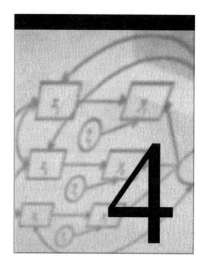

4

4.1 Introduction

Many response variables are counts of something: number of articles published by scientists, number of sex partners in the last year, number of arrests in a one-year period, number of students enrolled in a class, and so on. Some data analysts still treat count variables as continuous measures and apply ordinary linear regression. But that practice ignores two facts: the data are really discrete, and the distributions of count variables are typically highly skewed. For these reasons, it may be inappropriate to use models that assume normally distributed errors.

Nowadays, it's becoming increasingly popular to estimate Poisson regression models or negative binomial regression models, both of which are explicitly designed to model count data. In this chapter we'll see how to extend these count data methods to handle multiple observations per individual, with the inclusion of fixed effects to control for all stable predictor variables. Along the way, we'll revisit many of the issues that arose for dichotomous outcomes in chapter 3, although the problems encountered there turn out to be less serious for count data models.

Let's begin by describing the example that will carry us through the chapter. The data consist of 346 manufacturing firms with yearly counts of patents received in each of the years from 1975 through 1979. These data were previously analyzed by Hall, Griliches, and Hausman (1986) and later by Cameron and Trivedi (1998). There is one record per firm, with variables PAT75 through PAT79 containing the patent counts for the five years. As predictors we have the logarithm of research and development expenditures for each year from 1970 through 1979 (LOGR70 through LOGR79). There are also two time-invariant predictors: LOGSIZE, which is the natural logarithm of the book value of the firm in 1972, and SCIENCE, an indicator variable equal to 1 if the firm is in the science sector, and otherwise equal to 0.

4.2 Poisson Models for Count Data with Two Observations Per Individual

When there are only two observations per individual, we saw previously that a linear or logistic fixed effects analysis could be done using simplified methods with conventional software. This is also true for count data. In fact, a fixed effects Poisson regression model can be estimated with an ordinary logistic regression program.

For the patent data, let's ignore the intervening years and focus only on 1975 and 1979. Let y_{i1} be the patent count for firm i in 1975 and y_{i2} the patent count in 1979. We assume that each of these variables has a Poisson distribution with parameter λ_{it}. That is, the probability that $y_{it} = r$ is given by

$$\Pr(y_{it} = r) = \frac{\lambda_{it}^r e^{-\lambda_{it}}}{r!}, \qquad r = 0, 1, 2, \ldots \tag{4.1}$$

Why a Poisson distribution? Well, the Poisson distribution is perhaps the simplest probability distribution that is appropriate for count data. It can be derived from a stochastic process in which it is assumed that events (in this case patents) cannot occur simultaneously, and that events are independent (Cameron and Trivedi 1998). That is, the occurrence of an event neither raises nor lowers the probability of future events. Note that we are not assuming that there is a single Poisson distribution for the entire sample. Instead, each firm's patent count is drawn from a different Poisson distribution whose parameter λ_{it} varies across both firms and time.

An important property of the Poisson distribution is that its mean and variance are equal, and both are equal to the Poisson parameter:

$$E(y_{it}) = \text{var}(y_{it}) = \lambda_{it} \tag{4.2}$$

Next, we let λ_{it} be a log-linear function of the predictor variables:

$$\log \lambda_{it} = \mu_t + \beta x_{it} + \gamma z_i + \alpha_i \tag{4.3}$$

As in earlier chapters, x_{it} represents the time-varying predictor variables, z_i denotes the time-invariant predictors, and α_i denotes the unobserved fixed effects. The vector x_{it} includes the R & D expenditures in the current year t and in each of the preceding five years.

Our goal is to estimate the parameters in equation (4.3). To do this, we shall use conditional maximum likelihood, the same method used in chapter 3 to estimate the fixed effects logistic regression model. Consider the distribution of y_{i2} conditional on the total event count for the two time periods combined, denoted by $w_i = y_{i1} + y_{i2}$. It can be shown that $y_{i2}|w_i \sim B(p_i, w_i)$.

That is, conditional on the total count w_i, the 1979 count y_{i2} has a binomial distribution with parameters p_i and w_i, where

$$p_i = \frac{\lambda_{i2}}{\lambda_{i2} + \lambda_{i1}} \tag{4.4}$$

It follows, after a bit of algebra, that

$$\log\left(\frac{p_i}{1-p_i}\right) = (\mu_2 - \mu_1) + \beta(x_{i2} - x_{i1}) \tag{4.5}$$

Thus, we have converted our Poisson regression model into a logistic regression model in which the predictor variables are difference scores for the original predictors. Note that, as in earlier applications, both α_i and γz_i drop out of equation (4.5).

To implement this conditional approach in SAS, we may use any SAS procedure that does logistic regression for grouped data, including LOGISTIC, GENMOD, CATMOD and PROBIT. Here's how to do it in GENMOD. First, we create a new data set that contains the total count for each firm and the difference scores for the research and development variables:

```
DATA patents;
    SET my.patents;
    total=pat75+pat79;
    rd_0=logr79-logr75;
    rd_1=logr78-logr74;
    rd_2=logr77-logr73;
    rd_3=logr76-logr72;
    rd_4=logr75-logr71;
    rd_5=logr74-logr70;
RUN;
```

RD_0 is the difference score for the same years in which the patents were counted, whereas RD_1 through RD_5 are difference scores for lags of one to five years.

Let's first estimate a model with no covariates:

```
PROC GENMOD DATA=patents;
    MODEL pat79/total = / DIST=B;
RUN;
```

Note that the dependent variable is expressed with the *events/trials* syntax, which tells SAS that PAT79 events occurred out of a possible TOTAL. As in chapter 3, DIST=B specifies that PAT79 has a binomial distribution whose default link function is logit (i.e., logistic). Results are shown in Output 4.1.

Output 4.1 Conditional Poisson Regression Model for Patents, with No Covariates

Model Information	
Data Set	WORK.PATENTS
Distribution	Binomial
Link Function	Logit
Response Variable (Events)	pat79
Response Variable (Trials)	total

Number of Observations Read	346
Number of Observations Used	300
Number of Events	11107
Number of Trials	23865
Number of Invalid Responses	46

Criteria For Assessing Goodness Of Fit			
Criterion	DF	Value	Value/DF
Deviance	299	1001.3656	3.3490
Scaled Deviance	299	1001.3656	3.3490
Pearson Chi-Square	299	938.2458	3.1379
Scaled Pearson X2	299	938.2458	3.1379
Log Likelihood		-16484.8031	

Analysis Of Parameter Estimates

Parameter	DF	Estimate	Standard Error	Wald 95% Confidence Limits		Chi-Square	Pr > ChiSq
Intercept	1	-0.1386	0.0130	-0.1640	-0.1131	114.03	<.0001
Scale	0	1.0000	0.0000	1.0000	1.0000		

Under "Model Information" we see that 46 firms had invalid response values. These are firms that had 0 patents in both 1975 and 1979, so their total for the two years was also 0. Of course, the binomial distribution is undefined when the number of trials is 0, which is why these firms are excluded. This points out a more general characteristic of Poisson regression that extends to the next section as well. Whenever you condition on the total count, those cases that have a total count of 0 are effectively removed from the likelihood function. If the total is 0, then each component must also be 0, leaving no within-individual variability to analyze.

In the next panel, "Criteria for Goodness of Fit," we see that both the deviance and the Pearson chi-square statistics are more than three times their degrees of freedom. For a model to have a good fit, these statistics should be close to their degrees of freedom. However, because many of the expected counts generated by this model are small (near 0), the chi-square distribution may not be a good approximation. For that reason, it's probably not a good idea to compute a *p*-value. Nevertheless, the magnitude of these ratios suggests that there is a problem with *overdispersion*, about which I'll have more to say as the chapter progresses.

Finally, we get to the "Analysis of Parameter Estimates." The only estimate is the intercept, with a value of −.1386. What does this tell us? Well, if m_1 is the mean number of patents in year 1 and m_2 is the mean for year 2, the intercept is $\log(m_1/m_2)$. If the mean number of patents were exactly the same in both years, the intercept would be 0. The fact that it's negative indicates that the mean went down over time. More specifically, if we calculate $100(\exp(-.1386) - 1) = -12.9\%$, we get the percentage decrease in the mean from 1975 to 1979. Furthermore, because the chi-square for the intercept is so large, we can reject the null hypothesis that the means for the two years are the same. In effect, what we have here is the count data analog of the paired-comparisons *t*-test discussed in chapter 1, or the McNemar test for dichotomous variables discussed in chapter 3.

Now let's add the lagged variables for research and development expenditures as covariates, with results shown in Output 4.2. Again we see that the ratio of the goodness-of-fit chi-square statistics to their degrees of freedom is above 3, suggesting that we really need to do something about overdispersion. But let's postpone that issue for a moment. Examining the parameter estimates and their associated statistics, we see that RD_0, the contemporaneous measure of research and development expenditures, has a highly significant effect on the patent count, with a coefficient of .5214. To interpret this, keep in mind that both the dependent variable (expected number of patents) and the independent variable (research and development expenditures) are logged (see equation (4.3)). In that case, we can say that a 1% increase in R & D expenditures is associated with a .52% increase in the expected number of patents in the same year, controlling for the lagged R & D measures. The effects of the lagged measures are much smaller.

Output 4.2 Conditional Poisson Regression Model for Patents, with Covariates

Criteria For Assessing Goodness Of Fit			
Criterion	DF	Value	Value/DF
Deviance	293	949.3031	3.2399
Scaled Deviance	293	949.3031	3.2399
Pearson Chi-Square	293	890.2903	3.0385
Scaled Pearson X2	293	890.2903	3.0385
Log Likelihood		-16458.7718	

continued

Output 4.2 *(continued)*

				Wald 95%			
Parameter	DF	Estimate	Standard Error	Confidence Limits		Chi-Square	Pr > ChiSq
Intercept	1	-0.2225	0.0178	-0.2573	-0.1876	156.50	<.0001
rd_0	1	0.5214	0.0844	0.3561	0.6868	38.19	<.0001
rd_1	1	-0.2067	0.1129	-0.4280	0.0146	3.35	0.0671
rd_2	1	-0.1179	0.1110	-0.3355	0.0996	1.13	0.2880
rd_3	1	0.0601	0.0958	-0.1277	0.2478	0.39	0.5305
rd_4	1	0.1806	0.0900	0.0042	0.3569	4.03	0.0448
rd_5	1	-0.0932	0.0690	-0.2284	0.0420	1.83	0.1765
Scale	0	1.0000	0.0000	1.0000	1.0000		

Analysis Of Parameter Estimates

Now let's attend to the overdispersion problem. The big danger with overdispersion is that the standard errors may be underestimated, leading to chi-squares that are too large and *p*-values that are too low. There are several possible solutions to this problem, one of which is to formulate and estimate a model that directly builds in the overdispersion. One such model is the negative binomial model that will be discussed later in this chapter. But a simpler, though less elegant, approach is to correct the standard errors and chi-squares based on the goodness-of-fit ratios that alerted us to the problem. In PROC GENMOD, this is accomplished by using the DSCALE or PSCALE options on the MODEL statement. For example,

```
PROC GENMOD DATA=patents;
   MODEL pat79/total = rd_0-rd_5 / DIST=B DSCALE;
RUN;
```

The DSCALE option uses the deviance chi-square to make the adjustment while PSCALE uses the Pearson chi-square. The adjustment is very simple: Calculate the square root of the ratio of the chi-square statistic to its degrees of freedom. In Output 4.3 this number is reported as the "Scale" parameter in the last line. All standard errors are then multiplied by the scale parameter, which in turn attenuates the chi-squares and the *p*-values, as shown in Output 4.3.

Output 4.3 Conditional Poisson Regression Model with Overdispersion Adjustment

Criteria For Assessing Goodness Of Fit

Criterion	DF	Value	Value/DF
Deviance	293	949.3031	3.2399
Scaled Deviance	293	293.0000	1.0000
Pearson Chi-Square	293	890.2903	3.0385
Scaled Pearson X2	293	274.7858	0.9378
Log Likelihood		-5079.9585	

continued

Output 4.3 *(continued)*

Analysis Of Parameter Estimates

Parameter	DF	Estimate	Standard Error	Wald 95% Confidence Limits		Chi-Square	Pr > ChiSq
Intercept	1	-0.2225	0.0320	-0.2852	-0.1597	48.30	<.0001
rd_0	1	0.5214	0.1519	0.2238	0.8191	11.79	0.0006
rd_1	1	-0.2067	0.2032	-0.6050	0.1916	1.03	0.3091
rd_2	1	-0.1179	0.1998	-0.5095	0.2736	0.35	0.5550
rd_3	1	0.0601	0.1724	-0.2779	0.3980	0.12	0.7275
rd_4	1	0.1806	0.1620	-0.1369	0.4980	1.24	0.2649
rd_5	1	-0.0932	0.1241	-0.3365	0.1501	0.56	0.4527
Scale	0	1.8000	0.0000	1.8000	1.8000		

When this is done for the patent data, we find that only RD_0 retains its statistical significance, and even for this variable the chi-square is greatly reduced. Note also that the coefficients are not modified at all by this overdispersion correction. Other approaches to overdispersion—such as estimating a negative binomial model—might produce different coefficient estimates.

It's also possible to include predictor variables that do *not* vary with time, although the interpretation of their coefficients is not always straightforward. Output 4.4, for example, shows results for a model that includes the dummy variable for SCIENCE sector and the variable for LOGSIZE of the firm (while deleting the nonsignificant lagged R & D measures). Neither variable approaches statistical significance. Their coefficients can be interpreted as measuring interactions between each variable and time. Like all interactions, these coefficients can be interpreted in two ways. For example, the coefficient of .0275 for SCIENCE represents the *difference* between the coefficient for SCIENCE in 1979 and the coefficient in 1975. The fact that it is far from statistically significant suggests that this variable has the same the effect in both years. Alternatively, we can interpret .0275 as the increment in the effect of time for firms in the science sector, relative to those not in the science sector. Again, because it is far from significant, we may conclude that the rate of change in the number of patents from 1975 through 1979 is essentially the same for the two sectors.

Output 4.4 Conditional Poisson Model with Time-Invariant Covariates

Analysis Of Parameter Estimates

Parameter	DF	Estimate	Standard Error	Wald 95% Confidence Limits		Chi-Square	Pr > ChiSq
Intercept	1	-0.3335	0.1100	-0.5490	-0.1180	9.20	0.0024
rd_0	1	0.3770	0.1025	0.1761	0.5778	13.53	0.0002

continued

Output 4.4 *(continued)*

			Standard	Wald 95%			
Parameter	DF	Estimate	Error	Confidence Limits		Chi-Square	Pr > ChiSq
science	1	0.0275	0.0482	-0.0670	0.1219	0.33	0.5686
logsize	1	0.0161	0.0146	-0.0125	0.0448	1.22	0.2700
Scale	0	1.7961	0.0000	1.7961	1.7961		

Analysis Of Parameter Estimates

4.3 Poisson Models for Data with More Than Two Observations Per Individual

When there are more than two observations per individual, estimation of a fixed effects Poisson model in SAS is not so straightforward. Let's extend the example of the last section by analyzing annual patent counts from 1975 through 1979, with each count denoted by y_{it}. As before, we assume that y_{it} has a Poisson distribution given by equation (4.1) with parameter λ_{it}, and we let λ_{it} be the log-linear function of the predictor variables given in equation (4.3).

We'll consider two approaches to estimation—conditional maximum likelihood and unconditional maximum likelihood. In conditional maximum likelihood, the likelihood function is conditioned on the total count for each individual, thereby eliminating the fixed effects (α_i). The resulting conditional likelihood (Cameron and Trivedi 1998) is proportional to

$$\prod_i \prod_t \left(\frac{\exp(\mu_t + \beta \mathbf{x}_{it})}{\sum_s \exp(\mu_s + \beta \mathbf{x}_{is})} \right)^{y_{it}} \tag{4.6}$$

SAS has no procedure that is explicitly designed to maximize this likelihood. However, by directly specifying the likelihood function, it's possible to accomplish this with PROC NLMIXED. In chapter 3, we used NLMIXED to estimate random effects (mixed) models, which is what the procedure was designed for. But NLMIXED is also adept at estimating any model with a user-specified likelihood function. Here's how it's done for the patent data:

```
PROC NLMIXED DATA=my.patents;
   ARRAY pat [*] pat75-pat79;
   ARRAY rd [*] logr70-logr79;
   sum1=0; sum2=0; sum3=0;
   DO t=1 TO 5;
      j=t+5;
      eta=brd0*rd[j]+brd1*rd[j-1]+brd2*rd[j-2]+brd3*rd[j-3]+
          brd4*rd[j-4]+brd5*rd[j-5]+d1*(t EQ 1)+d2*(t EQ 2)+
          d3*(t EQ 3)+d4*(t EQ 4);
      sum1=sum1+pat[t]*eta;
      sum2=sum2+pat[t];
      sum3=sum3+EXP(eta);
   END;
   ll=sum1-sum2*LOG(sum3);
   MODEL pat79~GENERAL(ll);
   PARMS  brd0=.32 brd1=0 brd2=0 brd3=0 brd4=0 brd5=0 d1=0 d2=0
          d3=0 d4=0 ;
RUN;
```

Keep in mind that the MY.PATENTS data set used here has one record per firm, with the annual patent counts stored as separate variables in each record. The ARRAY statements create two arrays to hold the yearly counts of patents and the yearly measures of R & D expenditures. These are followed by three assignment statements that initialize to 0 the three sums needed in the construction of the likelihood function. The DO loop constructs the linear function of the covariate for each of the five years and accumulates the appropriate sums for constructing the log-likelihood. Note that the J=T+5 statement is needed here to align the different array lengths for patents and R & D measures. Note also the inclusion of four dummy variables (with coefficients D1 through D4) that allow the intercepts in 1975 through 1978 to differ from the intercept in 1979. The log-likelihood itself is defined in the line beginning LL. The MODEL statement specifies that PAT79 (it could have been any of the five response variables) has a distribution with log-likelihood LL. The PARMS statement sets starting values for all the parameters.

Results in Output 4.5 are similar to those we got in Output 4.2 using just two of the five years. That is, we find strong effects of R & D expenditures in the same year (BRD0), but much weaker effects for the lagged values (BRD1 through BRD5). The D1 through D4 coefficients show a tendency for patent counts to decline over the five-year period.

Output 4.5 Conditional Poisson Estimates for Five Years of Patent Counts

						Parameter Estimates				
Parameter	Estimate	Standard Error	DF	t Value	Pr > |t|	Alpha	Lower	Upper	Gradient
brd0	0.3222	0.04594	346	7.01	<.0001	0.05	0.2319	0.4126	0.011078
brd1	-0.08714	0.04869	346	-1.79	0.0744	0.05	-0.1829	0.008623	-0.00008
brd2	0.07859	0.04478	346	1.75	0.0802	0.05	-0.00949	0.1667	-0.00081
brd3	0.001053	0.04142	346	0.03	0.9797	0.05	-0.08040	0.08251	-0.0083
brd4	-0.00465	0.03785	346	-0.12	0.9023	0.05	-0.07909	0.06979	-0.00354
brd5	0.002616	0.03226	346	0.08	0.9354	0.05	-0.06083	0.06607	0.01007
d1	0.1980	0.01529	346	12.95	<.0001	0.05	0.1679	0.2281	-0.02576
d2	0.1554	0.01513	346	10.28	<.0001	0.05	0.1257	0.1852	-0.00123
d3	0.1580	0.01449	346	10.90	<.0001	0.05	0.1295	0.1865	-0.01514
d4	0.04092	0.01396	346	2.93	0.0036	0.05	0.01347	0.06837	0.039358

Now let's try unconditional maximum likelihood. This can be accomplished by estimating a conventional Poisson regression model with dummy variables for all the firms (less one). The first step is to restructure the data so that there is one record for each firm year:

```
DATA patents2;
   SET my.patents;
   ARRAY pat (*) pat75-pat79;
   ARRAY logr (*) logr70-logr79;
   id=_N_;
   sumpat=pat79+pat78+pat77+pat76+pat75;
   IF sumpat NE 0 THEN DO t=1 TO 5;
      j=t+5;
      patent=pat(t);
```

```
        rd_0=logr(j);
        rd_1=logr(j-1);
        rd_2=logr(j-2);
        rd_3=logr(j-3);
        rd_4=logr(j-4);
        rd_5=logr(j-5);
        OUTPUT;
    END;
  RUN;
```

As before, two arrays are created to hold the patent and R & D measures. Then we define an ID variable that has a common value for all the records for each firm. Next we sum the patent counts for the five years. This is necessary in order to test (in the subsequent IF statement) whether the sum is 0 and then to eliminate 22 firms whose sum is 0. If this is not done, the coefficients for the dummy variables for those firms will fail to converge.

For each firm whose patent sum is not 0, the DO loop produces five records. Each record contains a patent count, a contemporaneous R & D value, and five lagged values of R & D, along with any other variables already in the MY.PATENTS data set. The new data set has 1620 observations. Observations for the first four firms are shown in Output 4.6.

Output 4.6 Observations for the First Four Firms in the Restructured Data Set

Obs	id	t	patent	rd_0	rd_1	rd_2	rd_3	rd_4	rd_5
1	1	1	32	0.92327	1.02901	1.06678	0.94196	0.88311	0.99684
2	1	2	41	1.02309	0.92327	1.02901	1.06678	0.94196	0.88311
3	1	3	60	0.97240	1.02309	0.92327	1.02901	1.06678	0.94196
4	1	4	57	1.09500	0.97240	1.02309	0.92327	1.02901	1.06678
5	1	5	77	1.07624	1.09500	0.97240	1.02309	0.92327	1.02901
6	2	1	3	-1.48519	-0.68464	-0.15087	0.08434	-0.21637	-0.45815
7	2	2	2	-1.19495	-1.48519	-0.68464	-0.15087	0.08434	-0.21637
8	2	3	1	-0.60968	-1.19495	-1.48519	-0.68464	-0.15087	0.08434
9	2	4	1	-0.58082	-0.60968	-1.19495	-1.48519	-0.68464	-0.15087
10	2	5	1	-0.60915	-0.58082	-0.60968	-1.19495	-1.48519	-0.68464
11	3	1	49	3.67343	3.58542	3.52962	3.44199	3.40697	3.39054
12	3	2	42	3.77871	3.67343	3.58542	3.52962	3.44199	3.40697
13	3	3	63	3.82205	3.77871	3.67343	3.58542	3.52962	3.44199
14	3	4	77	3.88021	3.82205	3.77871	3.67343	3.58542	3.52962
15	3	5	80	3.90665	3.88021	3.82205	3.77871	3.67343	3.58542
16	4	1	0	0.43436	0.53714	0.48840	0.58779	0.48454	0.54340
17	4	2	0	0.33836	0.43436	0.53714	0.48840	0.58779	0.48454
18	4	3	1	0.36561	0.33836	0.43436	0.53714	0.48840	0.58779
19	4	4	0	0.43860	0.36561	0.33836	0.43436	0.53714	0.48840
20	4	5	0	0.42459	0.43860	0.36561	0.33836	0.43436	0.53714

Once the new data set has been constructed, estimation with PROC GENMOD is straightforward:

```
PROC GENMOD DATA=patents2;
   CLASS t id;
   MODEL patent = rd_0-rd_5 t id / DIST=POISSON ;
RUN;
```

Specifying ID as a CLASS variable implies that GENMOD will create a set of 323 dummy variables comparing each firm with the reference firm. Note that for the Poisson distribution, the default link function is the logarithmic, which is consistent with equation (4.3).

Results are shown in Output 4.7. This output shows the first five estimates for the ID variable, but there are 318 more estimates that are not shown. These estimates of the fixed effects are of little interest in themselves, but their inclusion in the model is necessary to control for all the stable covariates. They will be omitted from the output displays for later models.

Output 4.7 Unconditional Poisson Estimates for Five Years of Patent Counts

Criteria For Assessing Goodness Of Fit

Criterion	DF	Value	Value/DF
Deviance	1286	2807.9304	2.1835
Scaled Deviance	1286	2807.9304	2.1835
Pearson Chi-Square	1286	2709.6854	2.1071
Scaled Pearson X2	1286	2709.6854	2.1071
Log Likelihood		224169.5057	

Analysis Of Parameter Estimates

Parameter		DF	Estimate	Standard Error	Wald 95% Confidence Limits		Chi-Square	Pr > ChiSq
Intercept		1	2.8057	0.1851	2.4428	3.1686	229.64	<.0001
rd_0		1	0.3222	0.0459	0.2322	0.4123	49.19	<.0001
rd_1		1	-0.0871	0.0487	-0.1826	0.0083	3.20	0.0735
rd_2		1	0.0786	0.0448	-0.0092	0.1664	3.08	0.0793
rd_3		1	0.0011	0.0414	-0.0801	0.0822	0.00	0.9796
rd_4		1	-0.0046	0.0378	-0.0788	0.0695	0.02	0.9024
rd_5		1	0.0026	0.0323	-0.0606	0.0658	0.01	0.9356
t	1	1	0.1980	0.0153	0.1681	0.2280	167.64	<.0001
t	2	1	0.1554	0.0151	0.1258	0.1851	105.58	<.0001
t	3	1	0.1580	0.0145	0.1296	0.1864	118.82	<.0001
t	4	1	0.0409	0.0140	0.0136	0.0683	8.59	0.0034

continued

Output 4.7 *(continued)*

				Standard	*Wald 95%*			
Parameter		*DF*	*Estimate*	*Error*	*Confidence Limits*		*Chi-Square*	*Pr > ChiSq*
t	5	0	0.0000	0.0000	0.0000	0.0000	.	.
id	1	1	0.7417	0.1457	0.4560	1.0273	25.89	<.0001
id	2	1	-2.1747	0.4160	-2.9900	-1.3594	27.33	<.0001
id	3	1	0.0255	0.0921	-0.1550	0.2061	0.08	0.7818
id	4	1	-4.6540	1.0125	-6.6385	-2.6694	21.13	<.0001
id	5	1	-3.9906	1.0286	-6.0066	-1.9746	15.05	0.0001

Analysis Of Parameter Estimates

Comparing Output 4.7 with Output 4.5, we find that the coefficients for the R & D measures and for the time dummies are identical for the conditional and unconditional methods. Standard errors, chi-squares and *p*-values are also identical for these variables. Unlike logistic regression, for which conditional and unconditional estimates can differ substantially, these two methods always produce identical results for Poisson regression (Cameron and Trivedi 1998).

There may still be reasons for choosing one method over the other, however. It takes somewhat more computing time to do the unconditional estimation (although the difference was trivial for this example). The reason is that PROC GENMOD must repeatedly invert a large matrix to estimate coefficients for the dummy variables distinguishing different firms. Greene (2001) has shown that it's possible to do unconditional estimation without the computational burden of inverting a large matrix, but that would require significant modification of GENMOD's algorithms.

Although conditional maximum likelihood has a computational advantage, there are also some disadvantages. As we've seen, the programming for PROC NLMIXED is considerably more involved than that for GENMOD. More important, unconditional estimation with GENMOD gives us statistics for gauging overdispersion and easy ways to correct for it. In Output 4.7, for example, we see that both the deviance and Pearson chi-square are more than twice their degrees of freedom, a clear signal that overdispersion may be a problem. As in the previous section, we can correct for overdispersion by using either the PSCALE or DSCALE option on the MODEL statement. Using PSCALE (which adjusts the standard errors based on the Pearson chi-square), we get the results in Output 4.8. With this adjustment, the chi-squares for the covariates are cut in half, and the *p*-values rise substantially. It is now quite clear that lagged measures of R & D expenditures contribute little, if anything, to the prediction of patent counts beyond the contemporaneous measure.

Output 4.8 Unconditional Poisson Estimates with Overdispersion Correction

Criteria For Assessing Goodness Of Fit

Criterion	*DF*	*Value*	*Value/DF*
Deviance	1286	2807.9304	2.1835
Scaled Deviance	1286	1332.6265	1.0363
Pearson Chi-Square	1286	2709.6854	2.1071

continued

Output 4.8 *(continued)*

Criteria For Assessing Goodness Of Fit			
Criterion	DF	Value	Value/DF
Scaled Pearson X2	1286	1286.0000	1.0000
Log Likelihood		106389.4684	

Analysis Of Parameter Estimates

Parameter		DF	Estimate	Standard Error	Wald 95% Confidence Limits		Chi-Square	Pr > ChiSq
Intercept		1	2.8057	0.2688	2.2789	3.3324	108.99	<.0001
rd_0		1	0.3222	0.0667	0.1915	0.4529	23.35	<.0001
rd_1		1	-0.0871	0.0707	-0.2257	0.0514	1.52	0.2176
rd_2		1	0.0786	0.0650	-0.0488	0.2060	1.46	0.2267
rd_3		1	0.0011	0.0601	-0.1168	0.1189	0.00	0.9859
rd_4		1	-0.0046	0.0549	-0.1123	0.1030	0.01	0.9327
rd_5		1	0.0026	0.0468	-0.0892	0.0944	0.00	0.9556
t	1	1	0.1980	0.0222	0.1545	0.2415	79.56	<.0001
t	2	1	0.1554	0.0220	0.1124	0.1985	50.11	<.0001
t	3	1	0.1580	0.0210	0.1168	0.1992	56.39	<.0001
t	4	1	0.0409	0.0203	0.0012	0.0806	4.08	0.0434
t	5	0	0.0000	0.0000	0.0000	0.0000	.	.

The predictor variables in Output 4.8 are all time varying. Can we also include time-invariant covariates in the model? In the previous section, with only two observations per firm, we included two time-invariant covariates in the logistic regression model that was used for conditional estimation of the Poisson model. The coefficients of those variables were interpreted as interactions with time. In the present example, time-invariant covariates cannot be directly included in the model because they would be perfectly collinear with the dummy variables for firms. However, we can specify interactions between time-invariant covariates and time-varying covariates, including time itself. For example, one might hypothesize that R & D expenditures have a greater effect on patents in science-based firms than in other sectors. Here's a model to test that hypothesis:

```
PROC GENMOD DATA=patents2;
   CLASS t id;
   MODEL patent = rd_0 rd_0*science t id / PSCALE D=P ;
RUN;
```

For simplicity, this model deletes the lagged effects of R & D, which were not significant in Output 4.8.

Results in Output 4.9 show a significant interaction between RD_0 and the indicator variable SCIENCE, but the effect is opposite to the hypothesis; R & D expenditures have a greater impact on patent counts among non-science firms than in science firms. To be more specific, the effect of R & D for non-science firms is .3755, the main effect for RD_0. The effect for science firms is .3755 – .2038 = .1717, the main effect plus the interaction.

Output 4.9 Unconditional Poisson Estimates with Time-Invariant Covariate

Analysis Of Parameter Estimates

Parameter		DF	Estimate	Standard Error	Wald 95% Confidence Limits		Chi-Square	Pr > ChiSq
Intercept		1	3.2427	0.2739	2.7059	3.7795	140.19	<.0001
rd_0		1	0.3755	0.0691	0.2400	0.5110	29.49	<.0001
rd_0*science		1	-0.2038	0.0969	-0.3938	-0.0139	4.42	0.0355
t	1	1	0.1886	0.0222	0.1450	0.2322	71.88	<.0001
t	2	1	0.1541	0.0215	0.1119	0.1964	51.18	<.0001
t	3	1	0.1542	0.0203	0.1143	0.1940	57.42	<.0001
t	4	1	0.0380	0.0197	-0.0007	0.0767	3.70	0.0544
t	5	0	0.0000	0.0000	0.0000	0.0000	.	.

Now let's test whether the rate of change over time in patents is different for science and non-science sectors. The following program removes T from the CLASS statement to constrain the effect of time to be linear, and then includes the interaction between T and SCIENCE.

```
PROC GENMOD DATA=patents2;
   CLASS id;
   MODEL patent = rd_0 t t*science id / PSCALE D=P ;
RUN;
```

Results in Output 4.10 show no evidence for a difference between science and non-science firms in their rate of change over time. The interaction coefficient is far from statistically significant, and its magnitude is only about 2% of the main effect of time.

Output 4.10 Poisson Model with Interaction between Time and SCIENCE

Analysis Of Parameter Estimates

Parameter	DF	Estimate	Standard Error	Wald 95% Confidence Limits		Chi-Square	Pr > ChiSq
Intercept	1	3.1833	0.1918	2.8074	3.5593	275.43	<.0001
rd_0	1	0.2759	0.0573	0.1635	0.3883	23.15	<.0001
t	1	-0.0490	0.0071	-0.0629	-0.0352	48.14	<.0001
t*science	1	-0.0013	0.0085	-0.0179	0.0154	0.02	0.8801

4.4 Fixed Effects Negative Binomial Models for Count Data

As we just saw in the last section, Poisson regression models often run into problems with overdispersion. That's a bit surprising for fixed effects models because these models already allow for unobserved heterogeneity across individuals by way of the α_i parameters. But that heterogeneity is presumed to be time-invariant. There might still be unobserved heterogeneity that is specific to particular points in time, leading to observed overdispersion. As we've seen, the standard errors can be corrected for overdispersion by a simple method based on the ratio of the deviance (or Pearson chi-square) to its degrees of freedom.

Although that's not a bad method, we might do better by directly building overdispersion into the model for event counts. Specifically, we will now assume that the patent counts have a negative binomial distribution for each firm at each point in time. The negative binomial distribution can be regarded as a generalization of the Poisson distribution with an additional parameter that allows for overdispersion. The attraction of this approach is that the estimated regression coefficients might be more efficient (in the statistical sense), and the standard errors and test statistics might be more accurate than those produced by the simpler, after-the-fact correction method.

Negative binomial regression models can be formulated in different ways. The model we shall use here is what Cameron and Trivedi (1998) call an NB2 model. In this model, the probability mass function for y_{it} is given by

$$\Pr(y_{it} = r) = \frac{\Gamma(\theta + r)}{\Gamma(\theta)\Gamma(r+1)}\left(\frac{\lambda_{it}}{\lambda_{it}+\theta}\right)^r\left(\frac{\theta}{\lambda_{it}+\theta}\right)^\theta \tag{4.7}$$

In this equation λ_{it} is the expected value of y_{it}, θ is the overdispersion parameter, and $\Gamma(.)$ is the gamma function. As $\theta \to \infty$, this distribution converges to the Poisson distribution. As before, we assume a log-linear regression decomposition of the expected value,

$$\log \lambda_{it} = \mu_t + \beta x_{it} + \gamma z_i + \alpha_i \tag{4.8}$$

where the α_i are treated as fixed effects. Conditional on α_i, the multiple event counts for each individual (in this case, a firm) are assumed to be independent. But unconditionally, they may be dependent.

How can we estimate this model? Unlike the Poisson model, conditional likelihood is not an option here. In technical terminology, the total count for each individual is not a *complete sufficient statistic* for α_i, so conditioning on the total does not remove α_i from the likelihood function. Hausman, Hall and Griliches (1984) proposed a rather different fixed effects negative binomial regression model, and they derived a conditional maximum likelihood estimator for that model. In fact, their method has been incorporated into procedures in some widely available commercial software packages (not SAS). But Allison and Waterman (2002) have shown that this is not a true fixed effects regression model, and the method does not, in fact, control for all stable covariates.

Instead, we shall consider unconditional maximum likelihood estimation of models that include dummy variables for all individuals (except one). The following program estimates an unconditional negative binomial model in PROC GENMOD for the patent data.

```
PROC GENMOD DATA=patents2;
   CLASS t id;
   MODEL patent = rd_0-rd_5 t id / DIST=NB SCALE=0;
RUN;
```

The key difference with Poisson regression is the DIST=NB option on the MODEL statement. The SCALE option sets the starting value for the dispersion parameter. That option won't be necessary for most applications, but, in this case, the default starting value was not very good and the model failed to converge.

Results in Output 4.11 should be compared with those for Poisson regression in Output 4.7 (without overdispersion correction) and Output 4.8 (with overdispersion correction). It's apparent that the coefficients for the negative binomial model are very similar to those for the Poisson model. Moreover, the standard errors and test statistics for the negative binomial model are close to those for the Poisson model with overdispersion adjustment. (Note that the dispersion estimate reported in the last line of Output 4.11 is actually an estimate of $1/\theta$, where θ is the parameter in 4.7.)

Output 4.11 Fixed Effects Negative Binomial Regression Model

Criteria For Assessing Goodness Of Fit			
Criterion	DF	Value	Value/DF
Deviance	1286	1704.1804	1.3252
Scaled Deviance	1286	1704.1804	1.3252
Pearson Chi-Square	1286	1618.5570	1.2586
Scaled Pearson X2	1286	1618.5570	1.2586
Log Likelihood		224419.2756	

Analysis Of Parameter Estimates				Wald 95% Confidence Limits			
Parameter	DF	Estimate	Standard Error			Chi-Square	Pr > ChiSq
Intercept	1	2.5055	0.2809	1.9550	3.0560	79.56	<.0001
rd_0	1	0.3706	0.0634	0.2464	0.4948	34.22	<.0001
rd_1	1	-0.0827	0.0676	-0.2152	0.0499	1.49	0.2216
rd_2	1	0.0636	0.0641	-0.0621	0.1892	0.98	0.3214
rd_3	1	0.0136	0.0596	-0.1032	0.1305	0.05	0.8193
rd_4	1	0.0345	0.0565	-0.0763	0.1452	0.37	0.5420
rd_5	1	0.0018	0.0464	-0.0890	0.0927	0.00	0.9685
t 1	1	0.2237	0.0254	0.1738	0.2736	77.27	<.0001
t 2	1	0.1750	0.0251	0.1258	0.2241	48.69	<.0001
t 3	1	0.1722	0.0243	0.1246	0.2199	50.22	<.0001
t 4	1	0.0649	0.0235	0.0188	0.1110	7.62	0.0058

continued

Output 4.11 *(continued)*

					Wald 95% Confidence			
Parameter		DF	Estimate	Standard Error	Limits		Chi-Square	Pr > ChiSq
t	5	0	0.0000	0.0000	0.0000	0.0000	.	.
id	1	1	0.9477	0.2177	0.5210	1.3745	18.95	<.0001
id	2	1	-1.8294	0.4892	-2.7882	-0.8705	13.98	0.0002
id	3	1	-0.0103	0.1329	-0.2708	0.2502	0.01	0.9382
.				.				
.				.				
.				.				
id	344	1	-2.7074	0.5289	-3.7439	-1.6708	26.21	<.0001
id	345	1	1.0781	0.1957	0.6945	1.4616	30.35	<.0001
id	346	0	0.0000	0.0000	0.0000	0.0000	.	.
Dispersion		1	0.0196	0.0020	0.0156	0.0236		

Analysis Of Parameter Estimates

Because the Poisson model is a special case of the negative binomial regression model, we can compare the two by constructing a likelihood ratio chi-square statistic. This is accomplished by taking the difference in their log-likelihoods and multiplying by 2:

$$2(224419 - 224169) = 500.$$

With only 1 degree of freedom, this result is statistically significant by any standard. (Note that one cannot take differences in the deviance to construct this test because the deviance is computed differently for Poisson and negative binomial models). The implication is that we should reject the Poisson model in favor of the negative binomial model. Equivalently, we reject the hypothesis that $1/\theta$ is equal to 0.

There are a couple of things worth noting about this test. First, some readers will be puzzled by the fact that both of the log-likelihoods are positive, although log-likelihoods for these models must in fact be negative. The reason is that the log-likelihood reported in GENMOD is not the true log-likelihood, but differs from it by a constant that depends on the data. This implies that differences in the reported log-likelihoods will be the same as differences in the true log-likelihoods. The other thing to remember is that you can't compare the log-likelihood for the negative binomial model with the log-likelihood for the Poisson model with overdispersion correction (reported in Output 4.8). That's because the overdispersion correction rescales the log-likelihood as well as the standard errors and test statistics.

So the negative binomial model is clearly a better fit to these data than the Poisson model. But, unlike the Poisson model (where conditional and unconditional estimates must be identical), we have no guarantee that unconditional negative binomial estimation is resistant to the incidental parameters problem (discussed for the logistic model in chapter 2). Allison and Waterman (2002) investigated this question with Monte Carlo simulations. They found that the unconditional estimator did not show any substantial bias, even under conditions most likely to produce bias from incidental parameters. Their simulations also showed that negative binomial estimators had substantially smaller true standard errors than Poisson estimators. Furthermore, confidence intervals produced by the Poisson method, even with the overdispersion correction, tended to be much too small under many conditions.

In sum, negative binomial estimation seems substantially superior to Poisson estimation for many applications. Nevertheless, the simulations also showed that the negative binomial method produced confidence intervals that tended to be too small, although the undercoverage was not nearly as severe as for the Poisson. Under many conditions, nominal 95% confidence intervals covered the true value only about 85% of the time. This problem is easily corrected by using the DSCALE option in GENMOD (not the PSCALE option) to introduce additional correction for overdispersion. When this was done in simulations, the actual coverage rates were very close to the nominal 95% confidence intervals for nearly all conditions. Output 4.12 shows the results of applying the DSCALE correction to the model for the patent data. For this set of covariates, these estimates are the best among the various estimation methods we have considered.

Output 4.12 Fixed Effects Negative Binomial Model with Overdispersion Correction

Criteria For Assessing Goodness Of Fit

Criterion	DF	Value	Value/DF
Deviance	1286	1704.1754	1.3252
Scaled Deviance	1286	1286.0000	1.0000
Pearson Chi-Square	1286	1618.5521	1.2586
Scaled Pearson X2	1286	1221.3872	0.9498
Log Likelihood		169350.6376	

Analysis Of Parameter Estimates

Parameter		DF	Estimate	Standard Error	Wald 95% Confidence Limits		Chi-Square	Pr > ChiSq
Intercept		1	1.4442	0.1343	1.1810	1.7074	115.66	<.0001
rd_0		1	0.3706	0.0729	0.2277	0.5136	25.82	<.0001
rd_1		1	-0.0827	0.0779	-0.2352	0.0699	1.13	0.2884
rd_2		1	0.0636	0.0738	-0.0811	0.2082	0.74	0.3891
rd_3		1	0.0136	0.0686	-0.1209	0.1482	0.04	0.8427
rd_4		1	0.0345	0.0651	-0.0931	0.1620	0.28	0.5963
rd_5		1	0.0018	0.0534	-0.1028	0.1064	0.00	0.9726
t	1	1	0.0965	0.0175	0.0622	0.1309	30.38	<.0001
t	2	1	0.0478	0.0170	0.0144	0.0812	7.87	0.0050
t	3	1	0.0451	0.0167	0.0124	0.0778	7.29	0.0069
t	4	1	-0.0623	0.0171	-0.0958	-0.0288	13.28	0.0003

Although computation time for the unconditional negative binomial estimates was quite tolerable for the patent data, it could become a burden for very large data sets with lots of dummy variable coefficients to estimate. Again, Greene (2001) has shown how such computational difficulties can be readily overcome, but that would require modification of GENMOD algorithms.

4.5 Comparison with Random Effects Models and GEE Estimation

As we saw in chapters 2 and 3, random effects models and GEE estimation are widely used alternatives to fixed effects methods for longitudinal data. Both methods can be applied to count data and are readily available in SAS. The principal attractions of these alternative methods are (1) the ability to estimate effects for time-invariant covariates, and (2) more efficient use of the data (if the assumptions are met). The major disadvantage is that neither method controls for unmeasured time-invariant covariates. I'll briefly describe these methods in this section, both to serve as a point of comparison with the fixed effects methods and because they will be needed for the hybrid method discussed in the next section.

As we've seen before, GEE is a form of iterated generalized least squares that allows for correlations among the repeated observations for each individual. GEE is easily invoked with the REPEATED statement in PROC GENMOD, and can be used with either a negative binomial model or a Poisson model. Here's the SAS code for GEE estimation of a negative binomial model for the patent data, with separate records for each firm-year:

```
PROC GENMOD DATA=patents2;
   CLASS id t;
   MODEL patent= rd_0-rd_5 t / D=NB;
   REPEATED SUBJECT=id / TYPE=MDEP(4) CORRW;
RUN;
```

The TYPE=MDEP(4) option specifies that the correlation matrix for patent counts among the five years of observation has a "banded" structure. There is one correlation for counts that are one year apart, another correlation for counts that are two years apart, and so on. The correlation for counts more than four years apart is set to 0 (hence the 4 in MDEP(4)), but four years is the maximum distance for these data anyway. This imposed structure can be seen in the estimated "Working Correlation Matrix," requested with the CORRW option and shown in Output 4.13. I also tried other correlation structures, but the TYPE=UN (for unstructured) could not be fitted with these data. The TYPE=EXCH (for exchangeable) specifies that all the inter-year correlations are identical. Although this specification yielded similar results, it seems unnecessarily restrictive.

Output 4.13 GEE Estimates for a Negative Binomial Model

Working Correlation Matrix

	Col1	Col2	Col3	Col4	Col5
Row1	1.0000	0.7567	0.7349	0.6655	0.6909
Row2	0.7567	1.0000	0.7567	0.7349	0.6655
Row3	0.7349	0.7567	1.0000	0.7567	0.7349
Row4	0.6655	0.7349	0.7567	1.0000	0.7567
Row5	0.6909	0.6655	0.7349	0.7567	1.0000

Analysis Of GEE Parameter Estimates

Empirical Standard Error Estimates

Parameter		Estimate	Standard Error	95% Confidence Limits		Z	Pr > |Z|
Intercept		1.0839	0.0884	0.9106	1.2572	12.26	<.0001
rd_0		0.4969	0.1131	0.2752	0.7186	4.39	<.0001
rd_1		-0.0451	0.1162	-0.2728	0.1826	-0.39	0.6977
rd_2		0.1613	0.0855	-0.0063	0.3289	1.89	0.0593
rd_3		0.0729	0.0944	-0.1121	0.2579	0.77	0.4401
rd_4		0.1380	0.0735	-0.0061	0.2821	1.88	0.0605
rd_5		0.0247	0.0544	-0.0818	0.1313	0.45	0.6492
t	1	0.2326	0.0497	0.1351	0.3301	4.68	<.0001
t	2	0.1825	0.0465	0.0914	0.2736	3.93	<.0001
t	3	0.1855	0.0383	0.1104	0.2606	4.84	<.0001
t	4	0.1169	0.0403	0.0380	0.1958	2.90	0.0037
t	5	0.0000	0.0000	0.0000	0.0000	.	.

Parameter estimates in Output 4.13 are roughly similar to those in Output 4.12 for the fixed effects negative binomial model. But unlike the fixed effects method, two of the lagged R & D measures have GEE coefficients that approach statistical significance. Interestingly, the standard errors for the GEE estimates are generally larger than those for the fixed effects method, which is the opposite of what would ordinarily be expected.

Random effects models can be fitted with PROC NLMIXED for either the Poisson or negative binomial distributions. Let's first consider a Poisson model. As before, we begin by assuming that y_{it} has a Poisson distribution with expected value λ_{it}. As with the fixed effects model, we then assume that $\log \lambda_{it} = \mu_t + \beta x_{it} + \gamma z_i + \alpha_i$. Now, however, instead of treating α_i as a set of fixed constants, we assume that it is a random variable, normally distributed with a mean of 0 and a variance σ^2. We also assume that α_i is independent of all measured variables in the model, and that the y_{it} terms are independent of each other, conditional on i. Under these assumptions, NLMIXED produces maximum likelihood estimates of all parameters. Here's the code for the patent data:

```
PROC NLMIXED DATA=patents2;
lambda=EXP(int+brd0*rd_0+brd1*rd_1+brd2*rd_2+brd3*rd_3+brd4*rd_4
    +brd5*rd_5+d1*(t EQ 1)+d2*(t EQ 2)+d3*(t EQ 3)+
    d4*(t EQ 4)+alpha);
    MODEL patent~POISSON(lambda);
    RANDOM alpha~NORMAL(0,s2) SUBJECT=id;
    PARMS int=1 brd0=0 brd1=0 brd2=0 brd3=0 brd4=0 brd5=0 d1=0
          d2=0 d3=0 d4=0 s2=1;
RUN;
```

The statement that begins with LAMBDA defines the expected patent count as a function of the explanatory variables. Note the inclusion of ALPHA, which is the random, firm-level effect. The MODEL statement says that patent counts have a Poisson distribution with parameter LAMBDA. The RANDOM statement declares that ALPHA has a normal distribution with a mean of 0 and variance of S2. This variance is assumed to be constant across firms and across time. Alternatively, it could be written as a function of other variables simply by including another assignment equation similar to the one for LAMBDA.

This model took about 19 seconds to estimate on my computer, as compared with about a quarter second for the GEE model with PROC GENMOD. Results are shown in Output 4.14. The coefficients are roughly similar to those we just saw with GEE estimation, but the standard errors are quite a bit smaller. This is probably because the GEE estimates presumed a negative binomial distribution, whereas the random effects model presumes a Poisson distribution, which allows for less overdispersion.

Output 4.14 NLMIXED Output for a Random Effects Poisson Model

Fit Statistics	
-2 Log Likelihood	10410
AIC (smaller is better)	10434
AICC (smaller is better)	10435
BIC (smaller is better)	10480

				Parameter Estimates						
Parameter	Estimate	Standard Error	DF	t Value	Pr > |t|	Alpha	Lower	Upper	Gradient
int	0.8460	0.06729	323	12.57	<.0001	0.05	0.7136	0.9784	-0.26972
brd0	0.4762	0.04227	323	11.26	<.0001	0.05	0.3930	0.5593	0.043797
brd1	-0.00684	0.04797	323	-0.14	0.8867	0.05	-0.1012	0.08754	0.258257
brd2	0.1333	0.04473	323	2.98	0.0031	0.05	0.04532	0.2213	-0.08825
brd3	0.05825	0.04126	323	1.41	0.1589	0.05	-0.02291	0.1394	0.260459
brd4	0.02590	0.03761	323	0.69	0.4916	0.05	-0.04810	0.09989	-0.02615
brd5	0.07911	0.03100	323	2.55	0.0112	0.05	0.01812	0.1401	0.076259

continued

Output 4.14 *(continued)*

Parameter Estimates

Parameter	Estimate	Standard Error	DF	t Value	Pr > |t|	Alpha	Lower	Upper	Gradient
d1	0.2520	0.01422	323	17.72	<.0001	0.05	0.2240	0.2799	0.048431
d2	0.2053	0.01422	323	14.43	<.0001	0.05	0.1773	0.2333	-0.03654
d3	0.1962	0.01394	323	14.07	<.0001	0.05	0.1687	0.2236	0.030349
d4	0.06218	0.01378	323	4.51	<.0001	0.05	0.03507	0.08929	0.006942
s2	0.8169	0.07580	323	10.78	<.0001	0.05	0.6677	0.9660	0.149421

To get a fairer comparison, let's estimate a random effects negative binomial model. While this can also be done with PROC NLMIXED, it's a little tricky because the parameterization of the negative binomial distribution in NLMIXED is different from the one I've used here. NLMIXED labels the parameters N and p (Johnson and Kotz 1969) while I use λ and θ. The functional relationship is $N = \theta$ and $p = \theta / (\lambda + \theta)$. Here's how to set it up:

```
PROC NLMIXED DATA=patents2;
lambda=EXP(int+brd0*rd_0+brd1*rd_1+brd2*rd_2+brd3*rd_3+brd4*rd_4
    +brd5*rd_5+d1*(t EQ 1)+d2*(t EQ 2)+d3*(t EQ 3)+
    d4*(t EQ 4)+alpha);
    MODEL patent~NEGBIN(theta,(theta/(lambda+theta)));
    RANDOM alpha~NORMAL(0,s2) SUBJECT=id;
    PARMS int=1 brd0=0 brd1=0 brd2=0 brd3=0 brd4=0 brd5=0 d1=0
        d2=0 d3=0 d4=0 s2=1 theta=1;
RUN;
```

Results are shown in Output 4.15.

Output 4.15 NLMIXED Output for a Random Effects Negative Binomial Model

Fit Statistics	
-2 Log Likelihood	9703.9
AIC (smaller is better)	9729.9
AICC (smaller is better)	9730.1
BIC (smaller is better)	9779.0

Parameter Estimates

Parameter	Estimate	Standard Error	DF	t Value	Pr > |t|	Alpha	Lower	Upper	Gradient
int	0.7069	0.06960	323	10.16	<.0001	0.05	0.5699	0.8438	-0.01105
brd0	0.5021	0.06226	323	8.06	<.0001	0.05	0.3796	0.6245	0.024034
brd1	-0.01835	0.07302	323	-0.25	0.8018	0.05	-0.1620	0.1253	0.015229
brd2	0.1205	0.06923	323	1.74	0.0828	0.05	-0.01573	0.2567	0.026795

continued

Output 4.15 *(continued)*

				Parameter Estimates					
Parameter	Estimate	Standard Error	DF	t Value	Pr > |t|	Alpha	Lower	Upper	Gradient
brd3	0.06403	0.06473	323	0.99	0.3233	0.05	-0.06331	0.1914	0.020925
brd4	0.1044	0.06142	323	1.70	0.0901	0.05	-0.01642	0.2252	0.057457
brd5	0.07823	0.04764	323	1.64	0.1015	0.05	-0.01548	0.1720	0.08812
d1	0.2802	0.02719	323	10.31	<.0001	0.05	0.2268	0.3337	-0.00773
d2	0.2244	0.02722	323	8.24	<.0001	0.05	0.1708	0.2779	0.032592
d3	0.2074	0.02702	323	7.68	<.0001	0.05	0.1542	0.2606	-0.04431
d4	0.08709	0.02680	323	3.25	0.0013	0.05	0.03436	0.1398	0.006565
s2	0.7720	0.06956	323	11.10	<.0001	0.05	0.6351	0.9088	0.003151
theta	30.2799	3.0701	323	9.86	<.0001	0.05	24.2400	36.3199	0.000062

In Output 4.15, the coefficients are quite similar in magnitude to those in Output 4.14 for the Poisson model, but the standard errors are somewhat larger. These are about on par with those for the fixed effects negative binomial model in Output 4.12, but still not as large as those for the GEE estimates in Output 4.13. For this model, like the fixed effects model, the only significant R & D coefficient is for the contemporaneous year. A chi-square statistic for testing the Poisson random effects model versus the negative binomial random effects model can be obtained by calculating the difference in their –2 log-likehoods: $10410 - 9704 = 706$. With 1 d.f., this chi-square is highly significant, implying a strong preference for the less restrictive negative binomial model.

4.6 A Hybrid Approach

As we saw with linear models and logistic models, it's possible to combine the fixed effects and random effects approaches to get some of the virtues of each. As before, the first step is to calculate the mean of each time-varying predictor variable for each individual, and then calculate the deviations from those means:

```
PROC SORT DATA=patents2;
   BY id;
PROC MEANS DATA=patents2 NWAY NOPRINT;
   CLASS id;
   VAR  rd_0-rd_5;
   OUTPUT OUT=means MEAN=mrd_0 mrd_1 mrd_2 mrd_3 mrd_4 mrd_5;
DATA patcomb;
   MERGE patents2 means;
   BY id;
   drd_0=rd_0-mrd_0;
   drd_1=rd_1-mrd_1;
   drd_2=rd_2-mrd_2;
   drd_3=rd_3-mrd_3;
   drd_4=rd_4-mrd_4;
   drd_5=rd_5-mrd_5;
RUN;
```

The next step is to run a regression model with both the deviations and the means as predictor variables. To do this correctly, it's important to use an estimation method that allows for dependence among the multiple observations for each individual. The simplest approach is GEE with PROC GENMOD:

```
PROC GENMOD DATA=patcomb;
   CLASS id t;
   MODEL patent= drd_0-drd_5 mrd_0-mrd_5  t / DIST=NB;
   REPEATED SUBJECT=id / TYPE=MDEP(4) CORRW;
   CONTRAST 'FE VS. RE' drd_0 1 mrd_0 -1,drd_1 0 mrd_1 -1,
            drd_2 1 mrd_2 -1, drd_3 1 mrd_3 -1,drd_4 1 mrd_4 -1,
            drd_5 1 mrd_5 -1;
RUN;
```

Here I've specified a negative binomial distribution with an MDEP correlation structure. The CONTRAST statement produces a chi-square test of the null hypothesis that all the deviation coefficients are equal to all the corresponding mean coefficients.

Results are in Output 4.16. The coefficients for the deviation variables can be interpreted as if they were fixed effects estimates in the sense that they control for all stable covariates. In fact, they are quite close to the fixed effects coefficients of the R & D variables in Output 4.12. However, the GEE standard error estimates are somewhat larger than those from the unconditional fixed effects method. The coefficients for the means are generally quite different from the deviation coefficients, although none is statistically significant. Under the GEE and random effects models of the last section, the deviation and mean coefficients should be the same. The chi-square test of that assumption, reported at the end of the output, indicates that there is marginal evidence for rejection.

Output 4.16 GEE Estimates of the Hybrid Model

Analysis Of GEE Parameter Estimates

Empirical Standard Error Estimates

Parameter	Estimate	Standard Error	95% Confidence Limits		Z	Pr > |Z|
Intercept	1.0944	0.0876	0.9227	1.2661	12.49	<.0001
drd_0	0.3597	0.1223	0.1201	0.5994	2.94	0.0033
drd_1	-0.1158	0.1177	-0.3465	0.1149	-0.98	0.3252
drd_2	0.0529	0.0819	-0.1076	0.2134	0.65	0.5183
drd_3	-0.0287	0.0887	-0.2024	0.1451	-0.32	0.7465
drd_4	0.0273	0.0852	-0.1397	0.1943	0.32	0.7485
drd_5	-0.0775	0.0781	-0.2305	0.0755	-0.99	0.3209
mrd_0	-0.0490	0.8545	-1.7239	1.6258	-0.06	0.9542
mrd_1	1.0590	1.8618	-2.5902	4.7081	0.57	0.5695
mrd_2	-0.9196	1.9653	-4.7714	2.9322	-0.47	0.6398
mrd_3	-0.3526	1.5650	-3.4200	2.7148	-0.23	0.8218
mrd_4	1.3779	1.1420	-0.8603	3.6162	1.21	0.2276

continued

Output 4.16 *(continued)*

Analysis Of GEE Parameter Estimates

Empirical Standard Error Estimates

Parameter		Estimate	Standard Error	95% Confidence Limits		Z	Pr > |Z|
mrd_5		-0.2428	0.4805	-1.1846	0.6990	-0.51	0.6134
t	1	0.1924	0.0504	0.0935	0.2912	3.81	0.0001
t	2	0.1428	0.0492	0.0464	0.2391	2.90	0.0037
t	3	0.1537	0.0392	0.0769	0.2305	3.92	<.0001
t	4	0.1019	0.0411	0.0214	0.1823	2.48	0.0131
t	5	0.0000	0.0000	0.0000	0.0000	.	.

Contrast Results for GEE Analysis

Contrast	DF	Chi-Square	Pr > ChiSq	Type
FE VS. RE	6	12.99	0.0432	Score

The alternative to GEE is to implement the hybrid method in the context of a random effects model. Here's the PROC NLMIXED code for doing that, with results in Output 4.17:

```
PROC NLMIXED DATA=patcomb;
lambda=EXP(int+d0*drd_0+d1*drd_1+d2*drd_2+d3*drd_3+d4*drd_4+
    d5*drd_5+m0*mrd_0+m1*mrd_1+m2*mrd_2+m3*mrd_3+m4*mrd_4+m5*mrd_5
    +t1*(t EQ 1)+t2*(t EQ 2)+t3*(t EQ 3)+t4*(t EQ 4)+alpha);
    MODEL patent~NEGBIN(theta,(theta/(lambda+theta)));
    RANDOM alpha~NORMAL(0,s2) SUBJECT=id;
    PARMS int=1 d0=0 d1=0 d2=0 d3=0 d4=0 d5=0 m0=0 m1=0
        m2=0 m3=0 m4=0 m5=0 t1=0 t2=0 t3=0 t4=0 s2=1 theta=1;
RUN;
```

The coefficients for the deviation scores, along with their standard errors, are remarkably close to the fixed effects estimates in Output 4.12. This suggests that the random effects hybrid approach may be superior to GEE in replicating fixed effects results (as we found for logistic models in chapter 3), but beware. While PROC GENMOD took about a fifth of a second to run the GEE model, PROC NLMIXED took seven *minutes* to estimate the random effects model. For both of these methods I could also have included time-invariant variables like SCIENCE. I did not do so in order to maximize comparability with the fixed effects results.

Output 4.17 PROC NLMIXED Estimates of the Hybrid Model

Fit Statistics	
-2 Log Likelihood	9671.0
AIC (smaller is better)	9709.0
AICC (smaller is better)	9709.5
BIC (smaller is better)	9780.9

continued

Output 4.17 *(continued)*

Parameter Estimates

Parameter	Estimate	Standard Error	DF	t Value	Pr > |t|	Alpha	Lower	Upper	Gradient
int	0.6940	0.07057	323	9.83	<.0001	0.05	0.5552	0.8328	0.009595
d0	0.3745	0.06874	323	5.45	<.0001	0.05	0.2393	0.5097	-0.00483
d1	-0.08268	0.07341	323	-1.13	0.2609	0.05	-0.2271	0.06175	-0.00721
d2	0.05900	0.06976	323	0.85	0.3984	0.05	-0.07825	0.1962	0.002148
d3	0.009520	0.06492	323	0.15	0.8835	0.05	-0.1182	0.1372	0.00983
d4	0.04112	0.06181	323	0.67	0.5063	0.05	-0.08047	0.1627	0.005421
d5	-0.00224	0.05033	323	-0.04	0.9646	0.05	-0.1012	0.09677	-0.00302
m0	-0.1543	0.7641	323	-0.20	0.8401	0.05	-1.6576	1.3490	-0.02112
m1	2.0226	1.5748	323	1.28	0.2000	0.05	-1.0756	5.1208	0.011452
m2	-2.1181	1.7480	323	-1.21	0.2265	0.05	-5.5570	1.3208	0.07705
m3	-0.2077	1.5771	323	-0.13	0.8953	0.05	-3.3104	2.8951	-0.11503
m4	1.7695	1.2742	323	1.39	0.1659	0.05	-0.7373	4.2763	0.06146
m5	-0.4168	0.5980	323	-0.70	0.4864	0.05	-1.5933	0.7598	-0.00998
t1	0.2285	0.02864	323	7.98	<.0001	0.05	0.1722	0.2849	0.006028
t2	0.1791	0.02824	323	6.34	<.0001	0.05	0.1236	0.2347	0.00154
t3	0.1739	0.02745	323	6.34	<.0001	0.05	0.1199	0.2279	-0.00316
t4	0.06997	0.02659	323	2.63	0.0089	0.05	0.01765	0.1223	0.009996
s2	0.7530	0.06758	323	11.14	<.0001	0.05	0.6201	0.8860	0.004639
theta	32.1344	3.3315	323	9.65	<.0001	0.05	25.5802	38.6886	0.000046

4.7 Summary

Fixed effects models for count data can be estimated using either PROC GENMOD or PROC NLMIXED. When there are only two observations per individual, conditional maximum likelihood estimation of a fixed effects Poisson model can be implemented by converting the Poisson model into a logistic regression model for grouped data, with difference scores as independent variables. When there are more than two observations per individual, conditional maximum likelihood estimation of the Poisson model can be accomplished with PROC NLMIXED. Unconditional maximum likelihood can be done with PROC GENMOD using dummy variables to estimate the fixed effects. Fortunately, conditional and unconditional estimation of the Poisson model yield identical coefficients and standard errors. However, estimation with PROC GENMOD makes it easy to adjust for overdispersion, a problem that frequently occurs with Poisson models.

A more elegant approach to overdispersion is to estimate negative binomial models which include an overdispersion parameter. Conditional maximum likelihood is not an option for these models, however. Unconditional maximum likelihood can be done with PROC GENMOD using dummy variables for the fixed effects and an additional overdispersion correction using the DSCALE option.

Finally, a hybrid method allows for the estimation of fixed effects coefficients for time-varying predictors while also estimating the effects of time-invariant predictors. As in previous chapters, this is accomplished by decomposing each time-varying predictor as an individual-specific mean and a deviation from that mean. Both sets of variables are included in the regression model, along with any time-invariant predictors. To adjust for within-individual dependence, one can use either GEE estimation (using PROC GENMOD with the REPEATED statement) or maximum likelihood estimation of a random effects model (with PROC NLMIXED).

Fixed Effects Methods for
Event History Analysis

5.1 Introduction

In both the social and biomedical sciences, there is a great deal of interest in regression models for predicting the occurrence and timing of events. Medical researchers primarily study deaths, but they may also model such events as infections or tumor recurrences. Social scientists are interested in a wide array of events, including births, marriages, divorces, job terminations, promotions, arrests, residence changes, and so on.

Statistical methods for modeling events are often called *survival analysis* because they were originally developed by biostatisticians to analyze the occurrence of deaths. But I prefer the term *event history analysis*, commonly used among social scientists, because it more aptly expresses the generality of these methods, and because it is particularly appropriate for modeling *repeated events*, which are a major focus of this chapter.

To do an event history analysis, you need a set of *event history data*, which is simply a longitudinal record of when events occurred to some individual or sample of individuals. Here's an example that we'll use throughout this chapter. In the 1995 National Survey of Family Growth (NSFG), a representative sample of American women was asked to report information on the births of all children ever born to them (http://www.cdc.gov/nchs/nsfg.htm). In the version of the data used here, 6,911 women reported on 14,932 live births. For each of these births, I calculated a birth interval labeled DUR: the length of time (in months) from the current birth to the next birth, or until the interview date if no subsequent birth was observed. As potential predictors of these birth intervals, several variables characterize the current birth:

PREGORDR   Order of the birth (1 through 15)

MARRIED   1 if married at the time of the birth, otherwise 0

AGE   Mother's age (in years) at birth

PASST   1 if delivery was paid for, in part, by public assistance funds, otherwise 0

NOBREAST   1 if mother did not breast feed baby, otherwise 0

LBW   1 if low birth weight, otherwise 0

CAESAR   1 if birth was by Caesarian section, otherwise 0

MULTIPLE   1 if more than one baby born, otherwise 0

There is also a variable COLLEGE, which is equal to 1 if the woman had some college education (at the time of the interview), and is otherwise 0; and a variable BIRTH, which is equal to 1 if the interval ended in another birth, or 0 if the interval was terminated by the interview (a censored interval). Finally, there is a variable CASEID, which is an ID number that is common to all the birth intervals for the same woman. The goal is to estimate a regression model predicting the length of birth interval.

5.2 Cox Regression

The most popular method for analyzing event history data is Cox regression, named after its inventor, David Cox (1972), who introduced the *proportional hazards model* and the *partial likelihood* method for estimating that model. Before we discuss fixed effects analysis, it's essential to review this method.

Rather than directly modeling the length of the interval, the dependent variable in Cox regression is the *hazard,* or instantaneous likelihood of event occurrence. For repeated events, the hazard may be defined as follows. Let $N_i(t)$ be the number of events that have occurred to individual i by time t. The hazard for individual i at time t is given by

$$h_i(t) = \lim_{\Delta t \to 0} \frac{\Pr[N_i(t + \Delta t) - N_i(t) = 1]}{\Delta t} \tag{5.1}$$

In words, this equation says to consider the probability of one additional event in some small interval of time Δt. Then form the ratio of this probability to Δt, and take the limit of this ratio as Δt goes to 0. For repeated events, the hazard function is also known as the intensity function.

The next step is to model the hazard as a function of the predictor variables. Letting $h_{ik}(t)$ be the hazard for the kth event for individual i, a proportional hazards model is given by

$$\log h_{ik}(t) = \mu(t - t_{i(k-1)}) + \beta x_{ik} \tag{5.2}$$

where x_{ik} is a column vector of predictor variables that may vary across individuals and across events, β is a row vector of coefficients, $t_{i(k-1)}$ is the time of the $(k-1)$th event, and $\mu(.)$ is an unspecified function. In this model, the hazard of an event depends on the time since the most recent event. Later, we'll consider alternative ways of representing the dependence on time.

The method of partial likelihood makes it possible to estimate β without specifying anything about the function μ. For details on how this is accomplished, see Allison (1995). In SAS, partial likelihood is implemented with PROC PHREG. Here's a program for estimating the model in (5.2), *without* incorporating fixed effects:

```
PROC PHREG DATA=my.nsfg;
   MODEL dur*birth(0)=pregordr age married passt
         nobreast lbw caesar multiple college / TIES=EFRON;
RUN;
```

In the MODEL statement, the left-hand side of the equation is expressed as DUR*BIRTH(0), which is necessary to allow for the fact that many of the intervals are terminated by the interview rather than by another birth. In event history terminology, these are called *censored* intervals. The variable BIRTH indicates whether or not an interval is censored, and the number in parentheses (in this case 0) gives the value of the variable that corresponds to censored cases. The TIES=EFRON option requests a slight technical change in the estimation method that I strongly recommend for routine use. See Allison (1995) for details.

In Output 5.1, we see that 6,911 of the birth intervals were censored. That's not surprising, because the data collection method implies that each woman's last interval was terminated by the interview. Looking at the "Analysis of Maximum Likelihood Estimates," we find that all the variables but one (low birth weight) have highly significant effects on the hazard for a subsequent birth. Increased hazards are associated with being married or being on public assistance. All the other variables have negative signs.

To get a more precise interpretation for the effect of each variable, it's helpful to look at the last column, labeled "Hazard Ratio." These numbers are the exponentiated values of the parameter estimates, and they are interpreted similarly to odds ratios in logistic regression. For example, MARRIED has a hazard ratio of 1.25. This means that women who are married at the time of a birth have a hazard for another birth that is 25% larger than the hazard for unmarried women (controlling for other variables in the model). The hazard ratio for MULTIPLE is .493, which means that if a woman has twins, the hazard for the next birth is cut in half. For AGE, the hazard ratio is .936, which means that each additional year of the mother's age *reduces* the hazard of a subsequent birth by $100(1 - .936) = 6.4\%$.

Output 5.1 Cox Regression Estimates for a Conventional Model

Model Information	
Data Set	MY.NSFG
Dependent Variable	dur
Censoring Variable	birth
Censoring Value(s)	0
Ties Handling	EFRON

continued

Output 5.1 *(continued)*

Summary of the Number of Event and Censored Values

Total	Event	Censored	Percent Censored
14932	8021	6911	46.28

Testing Global Null Hypothesis: BETA=0

Test	Chi-Square	DF	Pr > ChiSq
Likelihood Ratio	1702.5117	9	<.0001
Score	1607.4459	9	<.0001
Wald	1585.4544	9	<.0001

Analysis of Maximum Likelihood Estimates

Variable	DF	Parameter Estimate	Standard Error	Chi-Square	Pr > ChiSq	Hazard Ratio
pregordr	1	-0.16434	0.01150	204.0833	<.0001	0.848
age	1	-0.0006565	0.0000306	461.2265	<.0001	0.999
married	1	0.22320	0.02867	60.6010	<.0001	1.250
passt	1	0.13824	0.02868	23.2324	<.0001	1.148
nobreast	1	-0.27190	0.02332	135.9444	<.0001	0.762
lbw	1	-0.00246	0.04204	0.0034	0.9533	0.998
caesar	1	-0.11706	0.03054	14.6912	0.0001	0.890
multiple	1	-0.70661	0.14257	24.5635	<.0001	0.493
college	1	-0.20844	0.02598	64.3778	<.0001	0.812

Unfortunately, there's a potential problem with these results: 69% of the women contributed at least two birth intervals to the data set, and it's reasonable to suspect that there would be some dependence among these repeated observations. In particular, it's natural to suppose that some women have persistently short birth intervals, whereas others have persistently long intervals. The failure to address this dependence could lead to serious underestimates of the standard errors and *p*-values.

Fortunately, beginning with SAS 8.1, PROC PHREG includes an option called COVSANDWICH that makes it easy to correct for dependence when there are repeated observations. This option invokes a method variously known as the *robust variance estimator* or the *modified sandwich estimator*, developed for Cox regression by Lin and Wei

(1989) and described in some detail in Therneau and Grambsch (2000). Here's a modified PHREG program that includes this option.

```
PROC PHREG DATA=my.nsfg COVSANDWICH(AGGREGATE);
   MODEL dur*birth(0)=pregordr age married passt
         nobreast lbw caesar multiple college / TIES=EFRON;
   ID caseid;
RUN;
```

The option COVSANDWICH can be abbreviated to COVS. To correct for dependence, it's necessary to include both the AGGREGATE option and an ID statement that gives the name of the variable containing the ID number that is common to all observations in the same "cluster" (a woman, in this example).

Results are shown in Output 5.2. Looking first at the "Testing Global Null Hypothesis" panel, we find the score and Wald statistics now have two versions, "model-based" and "sandwich." The model-based chi-squares are the same as in Output 5.1, whereas the sandwich chi-squares have been adjusted for dependence among the observations. Clearly the adjustments have not been major. In the "Analysis of Maximum Likelihood Estimates," we see that the coefficient estimates and the hazard ratios are exactly the same as in Output 5.1. Robust variance estimation only affects the standard errors and associated statistics. The reported standard errors, chi-squares and p-values are all adjusted for dependence. We also get a new column "StdErr Ratio," which is the ratio of the corrected standard errors to the uncorrected standard errors in Output 5.1. For the most part, the corrections here are rather small. The one exception is the corrected standard error for PREGORDER, which is 37% larger than its uncorrected version, resulting in a corrected chi-square that is only about half the uncorrected statistic. It's still highly significant, however.

Output 5.2 Cox Regression with Robust Variance Estimation

Testing Global Null Hypothesis: BETA=0

Test	Chi-Square	DF	Pr > ChiSq
Likelihood Ratio	1702.5117	9	<.0001
Score (Model-Based)	1607.4459	9	<.0001
Score (Sandwich)	1503.1134	9	<.0001
Wald (Model-Based)	1585.4544	9	<.0001
Wald (Sandwich)	1575.6025	9	<.0001

Analysis of Maximum Likelihood Estimates

Variable	DF	Parameter Estimate	Standard Error	StdErr Ratio	Chi-Square	Pr > ChiSq	Hazard Ratio
pregordr	1	-0.16434	0.01575	1.369	108.8409	<.0001	0.848
age	1	-0.0006565	0.0000310	1.016	447.0998	<.0001	0.999
married	1	0.22320	0.02942	1.026	57.5589	<.0001	1.250
passt	1	0.13824	0.02952	1.029	21.9242	<.0001	1.148

continued

Output 5.2 *(continued)*

		Analysis of Maximum Likelihood Estimates					
Variable	DF	Parameter Estimate	Standard Error	StdErr Ratio	Chi-Square	Pr > ChiSq	Hazard Ratio
nobreast	1	-0.27190	0.02275	0.975	142.8908	<.0001	0.762
lbw	1	-0.00246	0.04298	1.022	0.0033	0.9543	0.998
caesar	1	-0.11706	0.02792	0.914	17.5824	<.0001	0.890
multiple	1	-0.70661	0.14371	1.008	24.1746	<.0001	0.493
college	1	-0.20844	0.02615	1.007	63.5451	<.0001	0.812

5.3 Cox Regression with Fixed Effects

Now we're ready to introduce fixed effects into the Cox regression model. As usual, this makes it possible to control for all stable predictor variables, while at the same time addressing the problem of dependence among the repeated observations. As in earlier fixed effects models, α_i represents the combined effects of all stable covariates:

$$\log h_{ik}(t) = \mu(t - t_{i(k-1)}) + \beta x_{ik} + \alpha_i \tag{5.3}$$

How can we estimate equation (5.3) for our birth interval data? One obvious possibility is to put dummy variables in the model for all women (except one). This method worked well for the Poisson and negative binomial regression models in chapter 4, but it runs into serious difficulties here. First, there is the practical problem of putting 6,910 dummy variables into a PROC PHREG model. I actually tried to do this, but my computer was still running after 10 days, at which point I terminated the job. In principle, such computational difficulties could be solved by using Greene's (2001) algorithms, but these are not currently available in any commercial software.

The more fundamental difficulty is the potential bias introduced by estimating so many "incidental parameters." In previous chapters, we saw that this bias could be quite serious for logistic regression models, but not for Poisson or negative binomial models. Elsewhere (Allison 2002), I've shown that Cox regression is more like logistic regression in this regard. When the average number of intervals per person is fewer than three, regression coefficients are inflated by approximately 30 to 90%, depending on the level of censoring (a higher proportion of censored cases produces greater inflation).

Fortunately, there is a simple alternative method that does the job very well. It's similar to the conditional likelihood methods used for both logistic and Poisson regression in that the coefficients for the dummy variables are not actually estimated but are eliminated from the likelihood function. First we modify equation (5.3) by defining

$$\mu_i(t - t_{i(k-1)}) = \mu(t - t_{i(k-1)}) + \alpha_i$$

which yields

$$\log h_{ik}(t) = \mu_i(t - t_{i(k-1)}) + \beta x_{ik} \tag{5.4}$$

In this equation, the fixed effect α_i has been absorbed into the unspecified function of time, which is now allowed to vary from one individual to another. Thus, each individual has her own hazard function, which is considerably less restrictive than allowing each individual to have her own constant.

Model (5.4) can be estimated by partial likelihood using the well-known method of stratification. Stratification allows different subgroups to have different baseline hazard functions, while constraining the coefficients to be the same across subgroups. It is accomplished by constructing a partial likelihood function for each subgroup, multiplying those likelihood functions together, and then maximizing the resulting likelihood function with respect to the coefficient vector β. In PHREG, stratification is implemented with the STRATA statement. Here's how it's done for the birth interval data:

```
PROC PHREG DATA=my.nsfg NOSUMMARY;
   MODEL dur*birth(0)= pregordr age married passt nobreast lbw
         caesar multiple college / TIES=EFRON;
   STRATA caseid;
RUN;
```

The statement STRATA CASEID creates a separate stratum for each value of CASEID, which means a separate stratum for each of the 6,911 women. That may seem like an enormous number of strata, but PHREG handles it with ease. The NOSUMMARY option is not essential, but it's strongly advised in order to avoid voluminous, uninformative output. If you don't include it, the output contains a line for each stratum, reporting the numbers of cases and events for that stratum.

The results in Output 5.3 show some noteworthy differences from those in Outputs 5.1 or 5.2. First, there's nothing reported for COLLEGE. Like most of our fixed effects methods, we can't estimate coefficients for variables that do not vary within person. Moving upward from COLLEGE, we see that the effect of a multiple birth is about the same as the previous estimates. But the coefficient for CAESAR is somewhat attenuated and no longer statistically significant. Low birth weight was previously far from statistically significant, but here the *p*-value is less than .01. The hazard ratio for LBW tells us that a low birth weight is associated with a 21% reduction in the hazard for a subsequent birth. The effect of breast feeding is attenuated, both in magnitude and significance. Public assistance was previously highly significant, but here it's not significant at all.   The effect of marital status is about the same. Age is no longer statistically significant. On the other hand, the effect of pregnancy order is *much* greater, both in magnitude and statistical significance. Each additional birth is associated with about a 50% reduction in the hazard for a subsequent birth.

Output 5.3 Cox Regression with Fixed Effects via Stratification

Testing Global Null Hypothesis: BETA=0

Test	Chi-Square	DF	Pr > ChiSq
Likelihood Ratio	2640.9583	8	<.0001
Score	2293.6193	8	<.0001
Wald	1855.3631	8	<.0001

Analysis of Maximum Likelihood Estimates

Variable	DF	Parameter Estimate	Standard Error	Chi-Square	Pr > ChiSq	Hazard Ratio
pregordr	1	-0.71663	0.03372	451.7316	<.0001	0.488
age	1	0.0000818	0.0001125	0.5285	0.4672	1.000
married	1	0.18307	0.06958	6.9219	0.0085	1.201
passt	1	0.07590	0.06863	1.2229	0.2688	1.079
nobreast	1	-0.12832	0.06047	4.5035	0.0338	0.880
lbw	1	-0.23642	0.08117	8.4832	0.0036	0.789
caesar	1	-0.07839	0.09272	0.7148	0.3979	0.925
multiple	1	-0.60731	0.21852	7.7240	0.0054	0.545
college	0	0	.	.	.	.

Why the differences? Well, like any fixed effects method, this one controls for all stable covariates, so it's possible that some of the earlier results in Output 5.2 were spurious. Thus, if I had to choose between the results in Output 5.2 and Output 5.3, I would emphatically choose the latter. The thing to keep in mind is that, in this analysis, each woman is being compared to herself in a different birth interval. For each woman, we're asking why some of her birth intervals are longer or shorter than others. Is it, for example, because she's married for some of the intervals and not for others? This approach will produce different answers than asking why some women tend to have longer birth intervals than other women.

This is particularly relevant to the PREGORDR variable. In a conventional Cox regression, this variable is likely to have a positive effect on the hazard for purely artifactual reasons. For a fixed interval of time, women who make it to higher numbers of births in that interval will necessarily have shorter birth intervals. By doing a fixed effects analysis, we are able to remove that artifact, which is why the negative coefficient becomes so much larger than before.

As with linear and logistic models, even though the fixed effects Cox model will not estimate the effects of time-invariant covariates like COLLEGE, it is possible to estimate interactions between time-invariant variables and other variables. For example, let's estimate a model that includes an interaction between COLLEGE and NOBREAST. Since PROC PHREG does not allow interactions to be directly specified in the MODEL statement,[1] it's necessary to create a new variable in a DATA step:

```
DATA nsfg2;
    SET my.nsfg;
    collbreast=college*nobreast;
PROC PHREG DATA=nsfg2 NOSUMMARY;
    MODEL dur*birth(0)=pregordr age married passt nobreast lbw
          caesar multiple collbreast / TIES=EFRON;
    STRATA caseid;
RUN;
```

Results are in Output 5.4. The interaction between COLLEGE and NOBREAST is statistically significant at the .05 level. But how is it interpreted? The main effect of NOBREAST represents the effect of this variable when COLLEGE=0, that is, among women without a college education. That coefficient is positive and far from statistically significant. The effect of NOBREAST among college-educated women is found by adding the main effect to the interaction $(-.2659 + .0421) = -.22$, which is statistically significant. The conclusion is that breast feeding increases the hazard of a subsequent birth among college-educated women, but not among other women.

Output 5.4 Fixed Effects Cox Regression with Interaction

Testing Global Null Hypothesis: BETA=0

Test	Chi-Square	DF	Pr > ChiSq
Likelihood Ratio	2645.5030	9	<.0001
Score	2296.1533	9	<.0001
Wald	1857.0837	9	<.0001

Analysis of Maximum Likelihood Estimates

Variable	DF	Parameter Estimate	Standard Error	Chi-Square	Pr > ChiSq	Hazard Ratio
pregordr	1	-0.71740	0.03373	452.4115	<.0001	0.488
age	1	0.0000777	0.0001126	0.4762	0.4901	1.000
married	1	0.18341	0.06955	6.9552	0.0084	1.201
passt	1	0.07536	0.06861	1.2064	0.2720	1.078
nobreast	1	0.04210	0.10019	0.1766	0.6744	1.043
lbw	1	-0.24208	0.08120	8.8879	0.0029	0.785
caesar	1	-0.07869	0.09277	0.7195	0.3963	0.924
multiple	1	-0.58926	0.21909	7.2334	0.0072	0.555
collbreast	1	-0.26590	0.12479	4.5402	0.0331	0.767

---

[1] In SAS 9, there is an experimental procedure called TPHREG that essentially duplicates PHREG with the addition of the CLASS statement. With this procedure, one can directly specify interactions on the MODEL statement.

5.4 Some Caveats

Despite the attractions of fixed effects Cox regression, it also has the usual disadvantages. As with other fixed effects methods we've employed, there may be a substantial loss of power compared with the conventional analysis. In this example, any woman with only one birth interval gets excluded because that interval can't be compared with any others. This eliminates 2,109 birth intervals. Second, among women with exactly two birth intervals, if the second interval (which is always censored) is shorter than the first, both intervals will be excluded. Here's why. Suppose the first interval is 28 months long, and the second interval is censored at 20 months. In constructing the partial likelihood for the birth that occurs at 28 months, the algorithm looks for other intervals (from the same woman) that are at risk of the event at that same time. But if the only other interval was censored at 20 months, the woman is no longer at risk of an observable birth at 28 months. As a result, there is nothing with which to compare the birth, and the woman is eliminated from the partial likelihood function. For the NSFG data, the elimination of these intervals results in the loss of another 1,468 cases.

Finally, even for those observations that are retained, the fixed effects method essentially discards information about variation *across* women and only uses variation *within* women. So if a particular covariate varies a great deal across women, but shows little variation over time for each woman, the coefficient for that variable will be poorly estimated. The variable PASST, for example, has 80% of its variance across women and only 20% within women. Not surprisingly, the standard error for its coefficient is more than twice as large in Output 5.3 as compared with Output 5.2, which was based on variation both within and between women.

Besides the usual limitations of fixed effects methods, fixed effects Cox regression is also susceptible to bias for certain kinds of variables. These problems are most likely to occur with the kind of data structure that occurs in the birth interval study. In that structure, individuals are observed for a fixed period of time and may have multiple events during that period, but only the last interval is censored. Chamberlain (1985) argued that this structure violates a basic condition of likelihood-based estimation because the probability that an interval is censored depends on the length of the previous intervals.

In a simulation study (Allison 1996), I showed that this violation does not create a serious problem for most predictor variables, but could lead to biases in estimating the effects of variables that describe the previous event history. In particular, fixed effects partial likelihood tends to find negative effects on the hazard for the number of previous events and the length of the previous interval, even when those variables do not have true effects. This is certainly consistent with the results in Outputs 5.3 and 5.4, which show strong negative effects of pregnancy order on the hazard of a subsequent birth. We should be very cautious in interpreting those effects, because they could potentially be an artifact of the method. This problem tends to be most severe when the average number of events per individual is low, and the proportion of intervals that are censored is high.

5.5 Cox Regression Using the Hybrid Method

In previous chapters, we saw that we could duplicate or closely approximate the results from a fixed effects analysis by decomposing the time-varying covariates into individual-specific means and deviations from those means, and then putting all the variables into a conventional regression analysis, possibly correcting for dependence among the multiple observations for each individual. Unfortunately, for reasons that are not clear, this approach does not seem to work well for Cox regression. For example, if the hybrid method is applied to the birth interval data, several of the variables have coefficients and *p*-values that are dramatically different from those shown in Output 5.3. My simulation studies of the hybrid method for Cox regression have also been discouraging. Accordingly, I cannot recommend the hybrid method for event history analysis.

5.6 Fixed Effects Event History Methods for Nonrepeated Events

Fixed effects Cox regression requires that at least some of the individuals in a sample experience more than one event, so that within-individual comparisons are possible. Obviously, then, the method cannot be applied to a nonrepeatable event like death. Nevertheless, under certain conditions, it may be possible to do a fixed effects analysis for nonrepeatable events by treating time as discrete and applying conditional logistic regression. In the epidemiological literature, this type of analysis is called a *case-crossover study* (Maclure 1991), although the implementation I describe here is a little different from the way that epidemiologists usually do it.

As usual, I begin with an empirical example. Suppose we want to answer the following question: Does the death of a wife increase the hazard for the death of her husband? That's a difficult question to answer with confidence, because any association between husband's death and wife's death could be due to the effects of common environmental characteristics. Most husbands and wives will have lived in the same house in the same neighborhood for substantial periods of time. Moreover, they will tend to have come from similar social and economic backgrounds and have similar lifestyles. Unless we can control for those commonalities, any observed association between the death of one spouse and the death of the other could be spurious. Hence, a fixed effects analysis is highly desirable as a way to control for all stable unmeasured covariates.

To answer our question, we have data on 49,990 married couples in which both spouses were alive and at least 68 years old on January 1, 1993. Death dates for both spouses are available through May 30, 1994. During that 17-month interval, there were 5,769 deaths of the husband and 1,918 deaths of the wife. We regard time as consisting of discrete units, in this case days, which we can enumerate as $t = 1, 2, 3, \ldots$. Let p_{it} be the probability that husband i dies on day t, given that he was still alive on the preceding day, and let $W_{it} = 1$ if the wife i was alive on day t, and otherwise 0.

We'll represent the effect of the wife's vital status on the probability of the husband's death by a logistic regression model

$$\log\left(\frac{p_{it}}{1 - p_{it}}\right) = \alpha_i + \gamma t + \beta W_{it} \tag{5.5}$$

where γt represents a linear effect of time on the log-odds on death, and α_i represents the fixed effects of all unmeasured variables that are constant over time. Note that no time-invariant covariates are included in the model because their effects are absorbed into the α_i term.

We will estimate the model by the method of conditional maximum likelihood, described in chapter 3, which eliminates the α_i terms from the estimating equations. Here's how it's done. For men who died, a separate observational record is created for each day that the couple is observed, from day 1 (January 1, 1993) until the day of death or the day of censoring. For each of these couple-days, the dependent variable Y_{it} is coded 0 if the man remained alive on that day, and coded 1 if he died on that day. Thus a man who died on June 1, 1993, would contribute 152 couple-days; 151 of those would have a value of 0 on Y_{it}, while the last would have a value of 1. The predictor variable W_{it} is coded 0 for all days on which the wife was alive and 1 for all days on which she was dead. No observations are created for men who did not die because, in a fixed effects analysis for dichotomous outcomes, individuals who do not change contribute nothing to the likelihood function. The model can then be estimated with PROC LOGISTIC as described in chapter 3.

Below is a SAS program to create the couple-day data set and estimate the model with PROC LOGISTIC. The original data set (MY.COUPLE) has one record per couple, with the following variables:

HDEAD	1 if husband died, otherwise 0
WDEAD	1 if wife died, otherwise 0
HDTIME	day of husband's death or day of censoring
WDTIME	day of wife's death or day of censoring
COUPLEID	a unique ID number for each couple

Here is the code for constructing the couple-day data set:

```
DATA coupleday;
   SET my.couple;
   WHERE hdead=1;
   DO day=1 TO hdtime;
      IF day = hdtime THEN husdead=1;
      ELSE husdead=0;
      IF wdtime<day THEN wifedead=1;
      ELSE wifedead=0;
      OUTPUT;
   END;
KEEP husdead wifedead day coupleid;
RUN;
```

The new data set, COUPLEDAY, has one record per couple per day, for a total of 1,377,282 records. Note that couples in which the husband did not die are excluded (as explained above). Next, we estimate a conditional logistic regression with PROC LOGISTIC:

```
PROC LOGISTIC DATA=coupleday DESC;
   MODEL husdead=wifedead day;
   STRATA coupleid;
RUN;
```

Unfortunately, this program produces the following warning messages:

```
WARNING: NRRIDG Optimization cannot be completed.

WARNING: The LOGISTIC procedure continues in spite of the above
         warning. Results shown are based on the last maximum
```

```
likelihood iteration. Validity of the model fit is
questionable.
```

```
WARNING: The information matrix is singular and thus the
         convergence is questionable
```

The reason for the convergence failure is that each couple's sequence of observations consists of a string of 0's on the dependent variable, followed by a 1. That is, the event always occurs at the last observation unit. As a consequence, any monotonically increasing function of time will perfectly predict the outcome for that person, making it impossible to get maximum likelihood estimates for that covariate or any other covariate in the model. In the logistic regression literature, this problem is known as *complete separation* (Albert and Anderson 1984; Allison 2003). Obviously, the problem would also occur if the covariate was the square root of time or the logarithm of time. On the other hand, it is possible to include non-monotonic functions of time such as $\sin(2\pi t/365)$, which would vary periodically over the course of a year.

Actually, for our mortality example, the problem of nonconvergence is not confined to the DAY variable. If we remove DAY from the model, we get the results in Output 5.5.

Output 5.5 Fixed Effects Event History Analysis with No Dependence on Time

Testing Global Null Hypothesis: BETA=0			
Test	Chi-Square	DF	Pr > ChiSq
Likelihood Ratio	259.4514	1	<.0001
Score	190.1588	1	<.0001
Wald	0.0436	1	0.8346

Analysis of Maximum Likelihood Estimates					
Parameter	DF	Estimate	Standard Error	Wald Chi-Square	Pr > ChiSq
wifedead	1	15.3441	73.5073	0.0436	0.8346

This time we don't get a warning message that the model has not converged, but that's misleading. The coefficient for WIFEDEAD is extremely large, with an even larger standard error, a telltale indication of convergence problems. Another warning sign is the huge disparity between the likelihood ratio chi-square and the Wald chi-square. The reason for these problems is the same as before. Because WIFEDEAD may increase with time but never decrease, it perfectly predicts the occurrence of a death on the last day. Consequently, the coefficient for WIFEDEAD gets larger at each iteration of the estimation algorithm.

One way to circumvent this problem is to redefine WIFEDEAD to be an indicator of whether the wife died within, say, the previous 60 days. This covariate increases from 0 to 1 when the wife dies, but then goes back to 0 after 60 days (if the husband is still alive). Estimating the model with varying windows of time can give useful information about how the effect of the wife's death starts, peaks and stops.

Here's the new code for a window of 60 days:

```
DATA coupleday;
   SET my.couple;
   WHERE hdead=1;
   DO day=1 TO hdtime;
      IF day = hdtime THEN husdead=1;
      ELSE husdead=0;
      IF 0<day-wdtime<60 THEN wifedead60=1;
      ELSE wifedead60=0;
      OUTPUT;
   END;
KEEP husdead wifedead60 day coupleid;
RUN;
PROC LOGISTIC DATA=coupleday DESC;
   MODEL husdead=wifedead60;
   STRATA coupleid;
RUN;
```

Based on the output from this code using several different windows of time, Table 5.1 gives estimated odds ratios for the effect of the wife's death on the husband's death. In all cases, the odds ratios exceed 1.0, and they are statistically significant for the 60-day interval and the 30-day interval. For the latter, the odds of the husband's death on a day in which the wife died during the previous 30 days are nearly double the odds if the wife did not die during that interval.

Table 5.1 Odds Ratios for Predicting Husband's Death from Wife's Death within Varying Intervals of Time

	Wife Died Within				
	15 days	30 days	60 days	90 days	120 days
Odds Ratio	1.26	1.96	1.61	1.27	1.26
p-value	.54	.006	.03	.24	.25

Although these results are certainly intriguing, the danger is that there is no control for change over time. This is not merely a technical problem, but one that can seriously compromise any conclusions drawn from a case-crossover study (Suissa 1995, Greenland 1996). For our example, if there is *any* tendency for the incidence of wife death to increase over the period of observation, this can produce a spurious relationship between the wife's death (however coded) and the husband's death. Intuitively, the reason is that the husband's death always occurs at the end of the sequence of observations for each couple, so any variable that tends to increase over time will appear to increase the hazard of the husband's death.

We now consider an alternative fixed effects method that appears to solve the problems that arise from uncontrolled dependence on time. Introduced by Suissa (1995), who called it the *case-time-control* design, the key innovation in this approach is the computational device of reversing the dependent and independent variables in the estimation of the conditional logit model. This makes it possible to introduce a control for time, something that cannot be done with the case-crossover method.

As is well known, when both the dependent and independent variables are dichotomous, the odds-ratio is symmetric: reversing the dependent and independent variables yields the same result, even when there are other covariates in the model. (This symmetry is exact when the model is saturated in the control covariates, but only approximate for unsaturated models.) In the case-time-control method, the working dependent variable is the dichotomous covariate—in our case, whether or not the wife died during the preceding specified number of days. Independent variables are the dummy variable for the occurrence of an event (the husband's death) on a given day and some appropriate representation of time, such as a linear function. Again a conditional logistic regression is estimated with each couple treated as a separate stratum. Under this formulation there is no problem with including time as a covariate, because the working dependent variable is not a monotonic function of time.

In Suissa's formulation of the method, it is critically important to include data from all individuals, both those who experienced the event and those who are censored. However, his model was developed for data with only two points in time for each individual, an event period and a control period. In that scenario, the covariate effect and the time effect are perfectly confounded if the sample is restricted to those who experienced events. On the other hand, censored individuals provide information about the dependence of the covariate on time, information that is not confounded with the occurrence of the event.

By contrast, our data set (and presumably many others) has multiple controls at different points in time for each individual. That eliminates the complete confounding of time with the occurrence of the event (the husband's death), making it possible to apply the case-time-control method to uncensored cases only. That's a real boon in situations where it is difficult or impossible to get information for those who did not experience the event. The only restriction is that when the model is estimated without the censored cases, one cannot estimate a model with a completely arbitrary dependence on time—that is, with dummy variables for every point in time.

Of course, if the censored cases are available (as in our data set), more precise estimates of the dependence on time can be obtained by including them. But even if censored cases are available, there is a potential advantage to limiting the analysis to those who experienced the event. The case-time-control method has been criticized for assuming that the dependence of the covariate on time is the same among those who did and did not experience the event (Greenland 1996). This criticism has no force if the data are limited to those individuals who experience events.

For the mortality data, the working data set is the same as before, with one record for each day of observation from the origin until the time of the husband's death or censoring. Because conditional logistic regression requires variation on the dependent variable for each conditioning stratum, we can eliminate couples in which the wife did not die before the husband, with no loss of information. Here is the DATA step to produce the observations for a 60-day window:

```
DATA coupleday2;
SET my.couple;
WHERE hdead=1 AND wdead=1 AND wdtime<hdtime;
DO day=1 TO hdtime;
   IF day = hdtime THEN husdead=1;
```

```
      ELSE husdead=0;
      IF 0<day-wdtime<60 THEN wifedead60=1;
      ELSE wifedead60=2;
      OUTPUT;
   END;
   KEEP husdead wifedead60 day coupleid;
   RUN;
```

This DATA step produced 39,942 couple-days, which came from only 126 couples. This is the number of couples in which the husband died *and* the wife died before the husband. Although this is a tiny fraction of the original sample of 49,990 couples, it's the only group that contains information about the effect of the wife's death on the husband's death using a fixed effects approach.

The working model is defined as follows. Let H_{it} be a dummy variable for the death of husband i on day t, and let P_{it} be the probability that the wife's death occurred within a specified number of days prior to day t. The logistic regression model is

$$\log\left(\frac{P_{it}}{1-P_{it}}\right) = \alpha_i + \beta_1 H_{it} + \beta_2 t + \beta_3 t^2 \tag{5.6}$$

This model allows for a quadratic dependence on time, although other functions could be used instead. Here is the program to do the estimation:

```
PROC LOGISTIC DATA=coupleday2 DESC;
   MODEL wifedead60=husdead day day*day;
   STRATA coupleid;
RUN;
```

Table 5.2 gives estimates of the odds ratios for varying windows of time. Results are quite similar to those in Table 5.2, which used the case-crossover method. Again, the evidence suggests that the effects of the wife's death on the hazard of the husband's death are limited in time, with considerable fading after about two months.

Although our working dependent variable is the wife's death, the odds ratios must be interpreted as the effect of the wife's death on the odds of the husband's death. That's because of the time ordering of the observations—the wife's death always precedes the husband's death. If the goal were to estimate the effect of the husband's death on the wife's mortality, we would have to construct a completely different data set that would include couple-days prior to the wife's death, but not thereafter.

Table 5.2 Odds Ratios for Predicting Husband's Death from Wife's Death within Varying Intervals of Time, Case-Time-Control Method

	15 days	30 days	60 days	90 days	120 days
Odds Ratio	1.26	2.08	1.74	1.28	1.11
p-value	.54	<.004	.01	.25	.63

In this example, we estimated the effect of a single dichotomous covariate (the wife's death within a specified number of days) on the occurrence of a nonrepeated event (the husband's death). The method enabled us to control for all stable covariates. But suppose we want to control for time-varying covariates, like smoking status. Simulation studies (Allison and Christakis 2000) indicate that additional covariates can simply be included as predictor variables in the logistic regression model specified in equation (5.6). Although the coefficients for any additional covariates would not be unbiased estimates of their effects on the husband's death, the introduction of such covariates will yield approximately unbiased estimates for the effect of the wife's death on the husband's death (β in equation (5.6)). If we want to estimate the effect of smoking status on the husband's death, then we must make the probability of smoking be the dependent variable in equation (5.6), possibly including the wife's vital status as a covariate. This procedure could work even if smoking status had more than two categories, in which case equation (5.6) would need to be specified as a multinomial logistic regression. However, I know of no way to generalize the case-time-control method to quantitative covariates (except as control variables).

5.7 Summary

Fixed effect regression analysis of event history data is easily accomplished when each individual has multiple, usually repeated, events. Like logistic regression, and unlike linear regression or Poisson regression, the use of dummy variables to represent the fixed effects typically leads to biased coefficient estimates for the other variables. Instead, the preferred method for fixed effects event history analysis is to do Cox regression with stratification to eliminate the fixed effects from the estimating equations. In PROC PHREG this is implemented by using the STRATA statement with a variable containing common ID numbers for each individual. This method is computationally efficient even for large numbers of strata and produces approximately unbiased estimates under most conditions.

As with other forms of fixed effects analysis, Cox regression with stratification can involve a substantial loss of statistical power. Of course, individuals with only one censored or uncensored observation contribute nothing to the analysis. Even individuals with one censored and one uncensored interval are eliminated if the censored interval is the shorter of the two. Finally, only within-individual variation is used in estimating the coefficients. For reasons that are not fully understood, the hybrid method, which worked well for linear, logistic and count data regression, does not produce correct results for Cox regression.

Serious difficulties arise in the attempt to do fixed effects regression analysis with nonrepeated events. The basic idea is to treat time as discrete and create a separate record for each discrete time point that is observed for each individual, from the beginning of observation to the time of the event or censoring. For each record, a dichotomous dependent variable is coded 1 if an event occurred at that time point, and otherwise is coded 0. Finally, one does a conditional logistic regression of this dependent variable with stratification on individuals, using predictors that vary across time points. The fundamental problem with this appealing approach is that if time (or any monotonic function of time) is used as a predictor, the model will not converge due to complete separation. The reason is that the event always occurs at the end of each individual's sequence of records, so time perfectly predicts the occurrence of the event.

Although models that do not include time can certainly be estimated, the resulting coefficient estimates might be biased because effects of time on both the hazard and the covariates have not been controlled. One solution is the case-time-control method, which appears to work well for a estimating the effect of a categorical covariate on the hazard. The innovation of this method is to reverse the role of the dependent and independent variables in the conditional logistic regression, making it possible to include time as a covariate in the model. Again, this is accomplished in SAS by using PROC LOGISTIC with stratification.

Linear Fixed Effects Models with PROC CALIS

6.1 Introduction

In chapter 2, we saw how to estimate fixed effects linear regression models using several different methods and several different SAS procedures, including REG, GLM, TSCSREG, GENMOD, and MIXED. Now we are going to estimate the same model with PROC CALIS, which is designed to estimate linear structural equation models with latent variables, sometimes known as LISREL models. Why do we need another SAS procedure when we already have five that will do the job? The reason is that by estimating the linear fixed effects model in CALIS, we can do several important things that are not possible with the other procedures:

- estimate models that are a compromise between fixed and random effects models

- construct a likelihood ratio test for fixed versus random effects

- estimate fixed effects models that include reciprocal effects of two response variables

- estimate fixed effects models with lagged values of the response variable

A separate chapter is devoted to this method because the data structure and the conceptual framework is quite different from that used for most of the methods described in chapter 2. I will first explain how to use PROC CALIS to estimate the random effects model described in chapter 2. Then we will see how that model can be modified to produce the fixed effects model.

6.2 Random Effects as a Latent Variable Model

In chapter 2, the random effects model was specified as

$$y_{it} = \mu_t + \beta x_{it} + \gamma z_i + \alpha_i + \varepsilon_{it} \tag{6.1}$$

where y_{it} is the value of the response variable for individual i at time t, x_{it} is a vector of time-varying covariates, z_i is a vector of time-invariant covariates, α_i denotes the random effects, and ε_{it} is a random disturbance term. We assume that α_i and ε_{it} represent independent normally distributed variables, each with a mean of 0 and a constant variance. We also assume, at least for now, that these random components are independent of both x_{it} and z_i.

It is now well known (Muthén 1994) that a random effects models such as the one in equation (6.1) can be represented as a structural equation model (SEM) that can be estimated with one of several software programs (e.g., LISREL, EQS, AMOS, or PROC CALIS). Conceptually, we regard equation (6.1) as specifying a separate equation for each point in time, with regression coefficients constrained to be the same across time points. The random components α and ε are regarded as latent variables; however, while there is only one α, there is a distinct ε for each time point.

SEM models are often represented as path diagrams (Kline 1998). Figure 6.1 is a path diagram for a model with three points in time and a single time-varying independent variable. In path diagrams for SEMs, the convention is that directly observed variables are enclosed by rectangles, whereas latent variables are enclosed by circles or ellipses. A straight, single-headed arrow denotes a direct causal effect of one variable on another, while a curved double-headed arrow denotes a bivariate correlation between two exogenous variables. (In the language of simultaneous equations, endogenous variables are those that are dependent variables in at least one equation. Exogenous variables are those that are not dependent variables in any equation.)

Figure 6.1 Path Diagram of a Random Effects Model for Three Points in Time

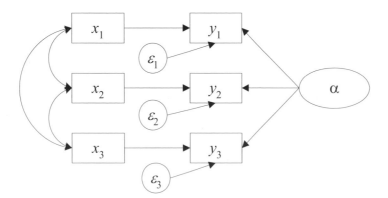

In chapter 2, we estimated the model in equation (6.1) using PROC MIXED for the NLSY data, which had observations at three points in time for 581 children. The working data set had three records per child, for a total of 1743 records. The dependent variable was a measure of antisocial behavior (ANTI). Independent variables included two time-varying variables, poverty (POV) and self-esteem (SELF), along with several time-invariant variables.

To estimate the model with PROC CALIS, we use the original form of the data set with one record per child and separate variable names for the same variable measured at different times. The model is specified as three distinct equations, one for each of the three time points, and each equation is a SAS language representation of equation (6.1). Here is the code:

```
PROC CALIS DATA=my.nlsy UCOV AUG;
LINEQS
   anti90=t1 INTERCEPT + b1 pov90 + b2 self90 +b3 black + b4
      hispanic + b5 childage + b6 married + b7 gender + b8 momage +
      b9 momwork + falpha + e1,
   anti92=t2 INTERCEPT + b1 pov92 + b2 self92 +b3 black + b4
      hispanic + b5 childage + b6 married + b7 gender + b8 momage +
      b9 momwork + falpha + e2,
   anti94=t3 INTERCEPT + b1 pov94 + b2 self94 +b3 black + b4
      hispanic + b5 childage + b6 married + b7 gender + b8 momage +
      b9 momwork + falpha + e3;
STD
   falpha e1 e2 e3 = s1 s2 s2 s2;
RUN;
```

Several things are worth noting about this program:

- The UCOV and AUG options are necessary for estimating a model with an explicit intercept. UCOV tells CALIS to estimate the model based on a sum of squares and a cross-products matrix rather than a correlation matrix. AUG says to augment this matrix with a column corresponding to a "variable" that has a constant value of 1.

- The LINEQS statement specifies the set of linear equations that make up the model. The equations are separated by commas and concluded with a semicolon.

- In each equation, names must be chosen for each of the parameters (b1, b2, etc.). If the same name is used in more than one equation, the corresponding parameter estimates are constrained to be equal.

- INTERCEPT refers to a "variable" with the constant value of 1. T1, T2 and T3 refer to the actual intercepts, which are allowed to differ across the three equations. This is equivalent to letting TIME be a CLASS variable in PROC MIXED.

- Variable names that are not on the input data set and which begin with an E, F, or D are assumed to be latent, unobserved variables. FALPHA, which appears in all three equations with an implicit coefficient of 1.0, corresponds to the α_i in equation (6.1). Similarly, E1, E2, and E3 correspond to the ε_{it} in equation (6.1).

- The STD statement assigns names to the variances of the latent variables and also imposes constraints. Thus, S1 is the variance of FALPHA, S2 is the variance of E1 and also the variance of E2 and E3. Setting those three variances equal is equivalent to the constant variance assumption.

As with most SEM programs, PROC CALIS produces a large amount of output. A small but crucial part of this output—the regression coefficients, standard errors and test statistics—is displayed in Output 6.1. Estimates are reported for each of the three equations, but because only the intercept is allowed to vary with time, most of this information is redundant. These estimates should be compared with those in Output 2.15 produced by PROC MIXED. The coefficient estimates are very close but, in some cases, differ slightly in the fourth or fifth decimal place. For example, the PROC MIXED coefficient for HISPANIC is –.2182, but for PROC CALIS it is –.2180. The reason for this difference is that the default estimation method in PROC MIXED is something called restricted maximum likelihood (REML), whereas the estimation method used in PROC CALIS is conventional maximum likelihood (ML). PROC MIXED can be forced to produce results that are identical to PROC CALIS by putting the option METHOD=ML on the PROC statement.

Another difference is that PROC CALIS produces three different intercepts, one for each point in time, whereas PROC MIXED gives one intercept and two coefficients for TIME. This difference is only apparent, however. The intercept reported by MIXED (2.741) is the intercept for time 3, which is close to the time 3 intercept in the CALIS output (2.748). To get the intercept for time 1, we add the coefficient for the time 1 dummy (–.2163) to the intercept, yielding 2.53, which is what PROC CALIS reports. Similarly, to get the intercept for time 2, we add the coefficient for the time 2 dummy (–.1690) to the intercept, yielding 2.579.

PROC CALIS also reports estimates of the variance of the latent variable, FALPHA, and the common variance for E1 through E3, as seen in Output 6.2. These are quite close to the covariance parameter estimates reported in Output 2.15 for PROC MIXED. Again, they would be virtually identical if we had used the METHOD=ML option on the PROC MIXED statement.

Output 6.1 Random Effects Model Estimated with PROC CALIS

```
              Manifest Variable Equations with Estimates

 anti90    =   -0.0219*momage    + -0.4834*gender    +   0.0885*childage
 Std Err        0.0252 b8            0.1060 b7            0.0907 b5
 t Value       -0.8709              -4.5602              0.9757

           + -0.2182*hispanic  +   0.2268*black     +   0.2611*momwork
             0.1376 b4              0.1251 b3            0.1142 b9
            -1.5861                1.8125               2.2875

           + -0.0496*married   + -0.0621*self90     +   0.2471*pov90
             0.1258 b6             0.00950 b2           0.0802 b1
            -0.3939               -6.5374               3.0813

           +  2.5314*Intercept +  1.0000 falpha     +   1.0000 e1
             1.0907 t1
             2.3209

 anti92    =   -0.0219*momage    + -0.4834*gender    +   0.0885*childage
 Std Err        0.0252 b8            0.1060 b7            0.0907 b5
 t Value       -0.8709              -4.5602              0.9757
```

continued

Output 6.1 *(continued)*

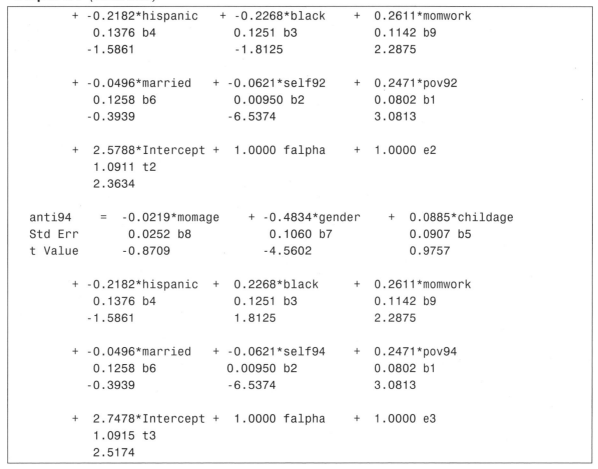

```
        +  -0.2182*hispanic   +  -0.2268*black    +   0.2611*momwork
           0.1376 b4             0.1251 b3             0.1142 b9
          -1.5861               -1.8125                2.2875


        +  -0.0496*married    +  -0.0621*self92    +   0.2471*pov92
           0.1258 b6             0.00950 b2            0.0802 b1
          -0.3939               -6.5374                3.0813


        +   2.5788*Intercept  +   1.0000 falpha    +   1.0000 e2
            1.0911 t2
            2.3634

anti94      =   -0.0219*momage    +  -0.4834*gender    +   0.0885*childage
Std Err          0.0252 b8            0.1060 b7             0.0907 b5
t Value         -0.8709              -4.5602                0.9757


        +  -0.2182*hispanic   +   0.2268*black    +   0.2611*momwork
           0.1376 b4             0.1251 b3             0.1142 b9
          -1.5861                1.8125                2.2875


        +  -0.0496*married    +  -0.0621*self94    +   0.2471*pov94
           0.1258 b6             0.00950 b2            0.0802 b1
          -0.3939               -6.5374                3.0813


        +   2.7478*Intercept  +   1.0000 falpha    +   1.0000 e3
            1.0915 t3
            2.5174
```

Output 6.2 Variance Estimates Produced by PROC CALIS for Random Effects Model

Variances of Exogenous Variables

Variable	Parameter	Estimate	Standard Error	t Value
falpha	s1	1.28489	0.09591	13.40
e1	s2	0.99458	0.04130	24.08
e2	s2	0.99458	0.04130	24.08
e3	s2	0.99458	0.04130	24.08

We now have a way of estimating a random effects model with PROC CALIS that gives us the same results as PROC MIXED. However, there are some important limitations to this method. First, unlike PROC MIXED, this method is difficult to implement with unbalanced data. That is, there must be the same number of repeated measurements on the outcome variable for each individual in the sample. If some of the children in our sample had missing values for, say, ANTI94, they would have to be deleted entirely from the sample. Second, although possible, it's quite cumbersome to set up the model to handle linear effects of time, linear interactions with time, or random coefficients (Muthén and Curran 1997). By contrast, this is easily managed in PROC MIXED. In PROC CALIS, it *is* easy to allow for unrestricted interactions with time by simply giving different parameter names to a variable's coefficients at different points in time.

Balancing these limitations are some important advantages to the SEM approach. First, it is possible to combine the random effects model with models for multiple indicators of latent variables. These variables may be either independent or dependent variables. Good introductions to latent variable models with multiple indicators can be found in Kline (1998) or Hatcher (1994). Second, as we will see in the next section, the random effects model in PROC CALIS can be extended to estimate fixed effects models in ways that facilitate a comparison and a compromise between the two models.

6.3 Fixed Effects as a Latent Variable Model

As noted in chapter 2, the basic random effects model is actually a special case of the fixed effects model (Mundlak 1978). The random effects model assumes that α_i is uncorrelated with x_{it}, the vector of time-varying covariates. The fixed effects model allows for *any* correlations between α_i and the elements of x_{it}. Figure 6.2 shows a path diagram for a simplified fixed effects model with a single time-varying predictor. The only difference between this diagram and the one in Figure 6.1 is the addition of the curved arrows representing correlations between α and the x variables.

Figure 6.2 Path Diagram of a Fixed Effects Model for Three Points in Time

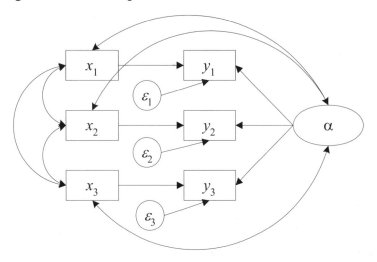

These additional correlations can be easily incorporated into SEM software such as PROC CALIS (Allison and Bollen 1997; Teachman et al. 2001). The default in CALIS is to assume that any latent variables are uncorrelated with all the observed predictor variables. To relax that assumption, we add the COV statement to our previous PROC CALIS program:

```
PROC CALIS DATA=my.nlsy UCOV AUG;
LINEQS
    anti90=t1 INTERCEPT + b1 pov90 + b2 self90 +b3 black + b4
        hispanic + b5 childage + b6 married + b7 gender + b8 momage +
        b9 momwork + falpha + e1,
    anti92=t2 INTERCEPT + b1 pov92 + b2 self92 +b3 black + b4
        hispanic + b5 childage + b6 married + b7 gender + b8 momage +
        b9 momwork + falpha + e2,
```

```
     anti94=t3 INTERCEPT + b1 pov94 + b2 self94 +b3 black + b4
        hispanic + b5 childage + b6 married + b7 gender + b8 momage +
        b9 momwork + falpha + e3;
STD
     falpha e1 e2 e3 = s1 s2 s2 s2;
COV
     falpha*pov90 pov92 pov94 self90 self92 self94 = c:;
RUN;
```

The COV statement allows a covariance (correlation) between FALPHA and each of the six variables representing the two time-varying explanatory variables, SELF and POV. The C: at the end of the statement says to name these covariances C1, C2, ..., C6. Note that a correlation cannot be allowed between FALPHA and any time-invariant predictors such as GENDER or MARRIED. Attempting to do so results in what is called an underidentified model, which may produce the following warning message in PROC CALIS:

```
NOTE: Covariance matrix for the estimates is not full rank.

NOTE: The variance of some parameter estimates is zero or some
      parameter estimates are linearly related to other parameter
      estimates as shown in the following equations:
```

The coefficient estimates and associated statistics for the fixed effects model are shown in Output 6.3. Only one equation is displayed because the other two are identical except for the intercept. Looking first at the coefficients for SELF and POV, we see that they are identical to the fixed effects estimates in Output 2.10, estimated with PROC GLM, and Output 2.21, estimated with PROC MIXED. The standard errors and *t*-statistics are also identical. Like the PROC MIXED results in Output 2.21, we also get estimates for the time-invariant variables. However, the estimates and test statistics in Output 6.3 for these variables are quite different from the estimates and test statistics in Output 2.21. For example, the coefficient for MOMWORK in Output 6.3 is clearly statistically significant, but is just as clearly not significant in Output 2.21. Why the difference? One clue is that when the mean scores for poverty and self-esteem (MPOV and MSELF) are removed from the model in Output 2.21, the results for the time-invariant variables, although not identical to those in Output 6.3, are quite close and certainly in qualitative agreement. This makes sense, because the CALIS model has no comparable variables to the mean scores (and, so far as I can tell, no way to include them).

Output 6.3 Fixed Effects Model Estimated with PROC CALIS

```
            Manifest Variable Equations with Estimates

anti90    = -0.0255*momage    + -0.4760*gender    + 0.0895*childage
  Std Err       0.0249 b8           0.1046 b7           0.0895 b5
  t Value      -1.0267             -4.5482             1.0001


         + -0.1976*hispanic   + 0.2688*black    + 0.2959*momwork
             0.1359 b4            0.1244 b3          0.1133 b9
            -1.4540              2.1606             2.6110
```

continued

Output 6.3 *(continued)*

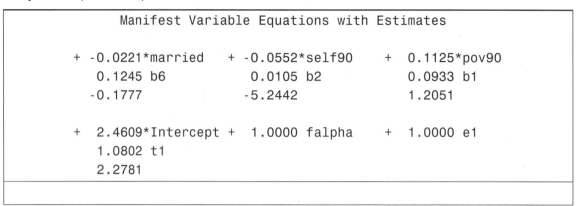

```
            Manifest Variable Equations with Estimates


   + -0.0221*married   + -0.0552*self90    +   0.1125*pov90
       0.1245 b6            0.0105 b2           0.0933 b1
      -0.1777             -5.2442              1.2051


   +  2.4609*Intercept +  1.0000 falpha    +   1.0000 e1
       1.0802 t1
       2.2781
```

Variances of Exogenous Variables

Variable	Parameter	Estimate	Standard Error	t Value
falpha	s1	1.30190	0.09751	13.35
e1	s2	0.99244	0.04121	24.08
e2	s2	0.99244	0.04121	24.08
e3	s2	0.99244	0.04121	24.08

Now that we have both a fixed effects and random effects version of our model in PROC CALIS, it is a simple matter to produce a likelihood-ratio statistic to compare them. For each model, the output contains a chi-square statistic and associated degrees of freedom. This statistic compares the overall fit of the model to a saturated model that perfectly reproduces the covariance matrix for all the variables. For the random effects model of Output 6.1, the chi-square is 84.4180 with 34 degrees of freedom. For the fixed effects model of Output 6.3, it's 66.4505 with 28 degrees of freedom. The difference between the two is a chi-square of 18.0305 and 6 degrees of freedom. The six degrees of freedom correspond to the six additional correlations that are allowed under the fixed effects model. The p-value for this chi-square is .006, indicating that we should reject the random effects model in favor of the fixed effects model. This is the same conclusion that we reached in chapter 2 using either the Hausman test produced by PROC TSCSREG or the tests of equality for coefficients of the mean and centered scores. (Both of those tests had 2 degrees of freedom.) From a theoretical point of view, however, the likelihood ratio test computed here is more elegant and might have better statistical properties. The Hausman test, for example, could have negative values for some data configurations, but this not possible for the likelihood ratio test.

6.4 A Compromise between Fixed Effects and Random Effects

In the previous section, we obtained a fixed effects model by starting with a random effects model and then allowing for all possible correlations between the random effect α and the time-varying explanatory variables. But perhaps all those correlations aren't really needed. Output 6.4 shows estimated correlations and covariances between α and the time-varying variables produced by PROC CALIS. It appears that the correlations with the SELF variables are very small and not statistically significant, whereas the correlations with the POV variables are somewhat larger, and two of the three are statistically significant. This suggests that we could set the SELF correlations equal to 0 without appreciably worsening the fit of the model.

Output 6.4 Correlations and Covariances of α and Time-Varying Variables

Correlations Among Exogenous Variables

Var1	Var2	Parameter	Estimate
self90	falpha	c4	-0.00569
self92	falpha	c5	-0.01407
self94	falpha	c6	-0.00756
pov90	falpha	c1	0.12273
pov92	falpha	c2	0.04911
pov94	falpha	c3	0.09536

Covariances Among Exogenous Variables

Var1	Var2	Parameter	Estimate	Standard Error	t Value
self90	falpha	c4	-0.13203	0.17203	-0.77
self92	falpha	c5	-0.33204	0.19404	-1.71
self94	falpha	c6	-0.18020	0.17811	-1.01
pov90	falpha	c1	0.08120	0.02429	3.34
pov92	falpha	c2	0.03216	0.02414	1.33
pov94	falpha	c3	0.06178	0.02477	2.49

This is easily accomplished by modifying the COV statement to eliminate the SELF variables, i.e.,

```
COV
  falpha*pov90 pov92 pov94 =c:;
```

This produces the results shown in Output 6.5. The coefficient and *t*-statistic for POV is about the same as for the fixed effects model in Output 6.3. On the other hand, the coefficient and *t*-statistic for SELF is somewhat larger than in the pure fixed effects model. Taking the difference in the chi-squares for the two models, we get a chi-square of 3.00 with 3 degrees of freedom. This is definitely not statistically significant, indicating that we cannot reject the simpler model (which set three correlations equal to 0) in favor of the more complicated model.

Output 6.5 Compromise Model Estimated with PROC CALIS

```
                  Manifest Variable Equations with Estimates


   anti90    = -0.0250*momage  + -0.4792*gender  +  0.0895*childage
   Std Err       0.0249 b8          0.1049 b7         0.0897 b5
   t Value      -1.0038           -4.5704            0.9987


          + -0.2017*hispanic  +  0.2686*black   +  0.2948*momwork
              0.1362 b4           0.1246 b3         0.1135 b9
             -1.4808             2.1550            2.5964


          + -0.0248*married   + -0.0622*self90  +  0.1114*pov90
              0.1248 b6          0.00947 b2        0.0931 b1
             -0.1984            -6.5706            1.1967


          +  2.5953*Intercept +  1.0000 falpha  +  1.0000 e1
              1.0791 t1
              2.4051
```

6.5 Reciprocal Effects with Lagged Predictors

We have seen that many of the fixed and random effects models estimated in chapter 2 can also be estimated with PROC CALIS, and that there are both advantages and disadvantages to this approach. We are now going to consider some important fixed effects models that go considerably beyond those in chapter 2. These models involve reciprocal effects among two or more endogenous variables as well as lagged values of both endogenous and exogenous variables. The models are important because they offer the possibility of greatly advancing our ability to determine the direction of causality among variables that are associated with one another.

Let's suppose that we observe two variables, x and y, that are known to be correlated, and we would like to know whether x causes y or y causes x (or perhaps both). Both variables are observed at several points in time. Consider the following model:

$$y_{it} = \mu_t + \beta x_{i(t-1)} + \alpha_i + \varepsilon_{it}$$
$$x_{it} = \tau_t + \delta y_{i(t-1)} + \eta_i + \upsilon_{it}$$

(6.2)

This model says that y is affected by x at an earlier time point, and x is affected by y at an earlier time point. The model also includes fixed effects α and η, representing the effects of any and all time-invariant covariates on each variable, along with time-specific disturbances ε and υ. Other lagged time-varying variables could be included, but that would unnecessarily complicate the discussion.

How can this model be estimated? If there are observations at exactly three time points, the model can be estimated by taking first differences and applying OLS to each equation separately:

$$y_{i3} - y_{i2} = (\mu_3 - \mu_2) + \beta(x_{i2} - x_{i1}) + (\varepsilon_{i3} - \varepsilon_{i2})$$
$$x_{i3} - x_{i2} = (\tau_3 - \tau_2) + \delta(y_{i2} - y_{i1}) + (\upsilon_{i3} - \upsilon_{i2})$$

(6.3)

When there are more than three time points, it might seem that the methods used in chapter 2 (dummy variables for individuals or deviations from the means) might do the job. Unfortunately, because of the reciprocal effects, the deviation scores used in fixed effects estimation are necessarily correlated with the error terms in the regressions, and that leads to biased estimation (Wooldridge 2001). Fortunately, the method used for handling fixed effects in PROC CALIS can circumvent those difficulties.

Even more serious difficulties arise when the model is extended to allow for lagged values of the dependent (endogenous) variables:

$$y_{it} = \mu_t + \beta_1 x_{i(t-1)} + \beta_2 y_{i(t-1)} + \alpha_i + \varepsilon_{it}$$
$$x_{it} = \tau_t + \delta_1 x_{i(t-1)} + \delta_2 y_{i(t-1)} + \eta_i + \upsilon_{it}$$

(6.4)

Without the fixed effects, this model is well known in the social science literature as the two-wave, two-variable panel model, or as the cross-lagged panel model. In the econometric literature, models with lagged dependent variables are referred to as *dynamic* models. They are known to pose serious difficulties for conventional estimation methods, and several alternative methods have been proposed to deal with them (Baltagi 1995)

It turns out that dynamic fixed effects models can also be estimated in a straightforward way using PROC CALIS (or equivalent SEM software). Although the properties of this method have not been investigated analytically, my own simulation studies (Allison 2000) have shown that it does an excellent job of recovering the parameters for models such as the one in equations (6.4).

As an example, we shall analyze data for 178 occupations in the U.S. for the years 1983, 1989, 1995 and 2001 (labeled T1 through T4). The data come from the March "Current Population Survey: Annual Demographic File" (CPS). The observations in CPS data are individuals, but the analysis is based on occupational averages for each year on all the variables. For each year, I calculated the proportion of females and the median wage for females for each occupation. This was done only for the 178 occupations that had at least 50 sample members in each of the years. Further details can be found in England et al. (2004). For wages, the variables are labeled MDWGF1 through MDWGF4, and for the proportion of females we have PF1 through PF4.

For the model in equation (6.4), let *y* be median wage and let *x* be the proportion of females. In 1983, the correlation between these two variables was –.33, which was highly significant. There has been considerable controversy regarding the possible direction of causality between these two variables (England et al. 2004). One argument is that employers devalue occupations that have a high proportion of females and consequently pay lower wages. The rival hypothesis is that declining wages make occupations less attractive to men; as they leave for better paying work, women fill their vacant positions. I shall assume that changes in either of these variables show up in changes in the other variable six years later.

By estimating the equations in (6.4), we can assess each of the two possible causal effects. Although it's possible to estimate the two equations simultaneously, estimating them separately allows for considerably more flexibility in specifying the model. In addition to the fixed effects, the key device that allows for the reciprocal effects is this: the error term at each point in time must be allowed to correlate with *future* values of the time-dependent covariate (Wooldridge 2001). Here is the PROC CALIS program to estimate the two equations:

```
PROC CALIS DATA=my.occ UCOV AUG;
LINEQS
    mdwgf4= t4 INTERCEPT + b1 pf3  + b2 mdwgf3 + falpha + e4,
    mdwgf3= t3 INTERCEPT + b1 pf2  + b2 mdwgf2 + falpha + e3,
    mdwgf2= t2 INTERCEPT + b1 pf1  + b2 mdwgf1 + falpha + e2;
STD
    falpha=s1, e2 e3 e4=sa:;
COV
    falpha*mdwgf1 pf1 pf2 pf3=ca:,
    e2*pf3 =cb;
RUN;
PROC CALIS DATA=my.occ UCOV AUG;
LINEQS
    pf4= t4 INTERCEPT + b1 mdwgf3 + b2 pf3 + falpha + e4,
    pf3= t3 INTERCEPT + b1 mdwgf2 + b2 pf2 + falpha + e3,
    pf2= t2 INTERCEPT + b1 mdwgf1 + b2 pf1 + falpha + e2;
STD
    falpha=s1, e2 e3 e4=sa:;
COV
    falpha*pf1 mdwgf1 mdwgf2 mdwgf3=ca:,
    e2*mdwgf3=cb;
RUN;
```

The basic structure of this program should now be familiar. There is a separate equation for each dependent variable at each point in time, and those equations correspond directly to the equations in (6.4). Note that there is no equation predicting median wage or proportion of females at time 1 because we do not observe their lagged values six years earlier (1977).

The fixed effects are represented by FALPHA in each equation. The COV statement allows correlations between FALPHA and the time-varying covariates, thus implementing a fixed effects model. Note that for the lagged dependent variable, a correlation is allowed only between FALPHA and the value of the variable at time 1. That's because only the time 1 variable is exogenous, and correlations are only allowed among exogenous variables. There's actually no need to specify a correlation between FALPHA and the later values of the lagged dependent variable, because FALPHA is one of the predictors in the equation for each of these variables. The COV statement also allows a correlation between E2 and the cross-lagged variable at time 3. Again, this allows for the reciprocal effect of one variable on the other at a later point in time.

Output 6.6 Estimates for Reciprocal Model with Fixed and Lagged Effects

```
                    Manifest Variable Equations with Estimates

mdwgf2    = -0.0836*pf1      +  0.3434*mdwgf1    +  7.9837*Intercept
  Std Err       2.4323 b1            0.0640 b2         1.2411 t2
  t Value      -0.0344              5.3680            6.4329

                   +  1.0000 falpha    +  1.0000 e2


pf2       =  0.2994*pf1      +-0.00054*mdwgf1    +  0.3353*Intercept
  Std Err       0.0820 b2            0.00151 b1        0.0384 t2
  t Value      3.6534               -0.3572            8.7220

                   +  1.0000 falpha    +  1.0000 e2
```

Results for the two equations are shown in Output 6.6. To save space, I've edited out everything that's redundant and nonessential. Not surprisingly, each variable has a positive, statistically significant effect on itself six years later. With respect to the "cross-lagged" coefficients, however, there is no evidence for an effect in either direction.

Elsewhere, I have questioned the desirability of including lagged values of the dependent variable as predictors when fixed effects are already in the model (Allison 1990). So I also estimated a model that removes the lagged dependent variables, and I got essentially the same results for the cross-lagged coefficients. Similarly, a model that includes the lagged dependent variables but does *not* include the fixed effects (the classic 2-wave, 2-variable panel model) yields no evidence for a cross-lagged effect in either direction.

6.6 Summary and Conclusion

Linear, fixed effects or random effects regression models for quantitative response variables can be estimated with PROC CALIS to yield the same results as those obtained using other SAS procedures as described in chapter 2. This method requires a different data structure, however, with one record containing all the measurements for each individual or cluster, and with the multiple measurements coded as distinct variables. In PROC CALIS, a separate equation is specified for each response variable at each point in time, and the coefficients are typically constrained to be the same across equations. The random or fixed effect is specified as a latent variable that is common to all the equations. In the fixed effects version, this latent variable is allowed to be correlated with all the predictor variables that vary across equations.

This approach is typically more cumbersome to set up than the methodology described in chapter 2. Nevertheless, it allows for a number of interesting extensions, including a likelihood ratio test comparing fixed and random effects, a compromise between fixed effects and random effects models, and models that have multiple indicators of latent variables. Most importantly, within PROC CALIS it is possible to estimate models for panel data in which two or more response variables are believed to have lagged, reciprocal effects on each other. Such models allow for much stronger causal inferences from nonexperimental data than is ordinarily the case.

References

Abrevaya, J. (1997), "The Equivalence of Two Estimators of the Fixed-Effects Logit Model," *Economics Letters*, 55, 41–44.

Agresti, A. (1993), "Distribution-Free Fitting of Logit-Models With Random Effects for Repeated Categorical Responses," *Statistics in Medicine*, 12, 1969–1987.

Albert, A. and Anderson, J. A. (1984), "On the Existence of Maximum Likelihood Estimates in Logistic Regression Models," *Biometrika*, 71, 1–10.

Allison, P. D. (1990), "Change Scores as Dependent Variables in Regression Analysis," in *Sociological Methodology 1990*, ed. C. Clogg, Oxford: Basil Blackwell, 93–114.

Allison, P. D. (1995), *Survival Analysis Using SAS: A Practical Guide.* Cary, NC: SAS Institute Inc.

Allison, P. D. (1996), "Fixed Effects Partial Likelihood for Repeated Events," *Sociological Methods & Research*, 25, 207–222.

Allison, P. D. (1999), *Logistic Regression Using the SAS System: Theory and Application.* Cary, NC: SAS Institute Inc.

Allison, P. D. (2000), "Inferring Causal Order from Panel Data," paper prepared for presentation at the Ninth International Conference on Panel Data, June 22, Geneva, Switzerland.

Allison, P. D. (2002), "Bias in Fixed-Effects Cox Regression with Dummy Variables," unpublished paper, Department of Sociology, University of Pennsylvania.

Allison, P. D. (2003), "Convergence Problems in Logistic Regression," in *Numerical Issues in Statistical Computing for the Social Scientist*, eds. M. Altman, J. Gill, and M. McDonald, New York: Wiley-Interscience, 247–262.

Allison, P. D. and Bollen, K.A. (1997), "Change Score, Fixed Effects, and Random Component Models: A Structural Equation Approach," paper presented at the Annual Meeting of the American Sociological Association.

Allison, P. D. and Christakis, N. (2000), "Fixed Effects Methods for the Analysis of Non-Repeated Events," unpublished paper, Department of Sociology, University of Pennsylvania.

Allison, P. D. and Waterman, R. (2002), "Fixed Effects Negative Binomial Regression Models," in *Sociological Methodology 2002*, ed. R. M. Stolzenberg, Oxford: Basil Blackwell, 247–265.

Baltagi, B. H. (1995), *Econometric Analysis of Panel Data.* New York: John Wiley & Sons.

Begg, C. B. and Gray, R. (1984), "Calculation of Polychotomous Logistic Regression Parameters Using Individualized Regressions," *Biometrika*, 71, 11–18.

Bryk, A. S. and Raudenbusch, S. W. (1992), *Hierarchical Linear Models: Application and Data Analysis Methods.* Newbury Park, CA: Sage.

Cameron, A. C. and Trivedi, P. K. (1998), *Regression Analysis of Count Data.* Cambridge, UK: Cambridge University Press.

Center for Human Resource Research (2002), *NLSY97 User's Guide.* Washington, DC: U.S. Department of Labor.

Chamberlain, G. (1980), "Analysis of Covariance with Qualitative Data," *Review of Economic Statistics*, 48, 225–238.

Chamberlain, G. (1985), "Heterogeneity, Omitted Variable Bias, and Duration Dependence," in *Longitudinal Analysis of Labor Market Data*, eds. J. J. Heckman and B. Singer, Cambridge, UK: Cambridge University Press, 3–38.

Conaway, M. R. (1989), "Analysis of Repeated Categorical Measurements With Conditional Likelihood Methods," *Journal of the American Statistical Association,* 84, 53–62.

Cox, D. R. (1972), "Regression Models and Life Tables" (with discussion), *Journal of the Royal Statistical Society, Series B*, 34, 187–220.

Darroch, J. N. and McCloud, P. I. (1986), "Category Distinguishability and Observer Agreement," *Australian Journal of Statistics*, 28, 371–388.

Diggle, P. J.; Liang, K. Y.; and Zeger, S. L. (1994), *Analysis of Longitudinal Data.* New York: Oxford University Press.

England, P.; Allison, P. D.; Wu, Y.; and Ross, M. (2004), "Does Bad Pay Cause Occupations to Feminize, Does Feminization Reduce Pay, and How Can We Tell with Longitudinal Data?" paper prepared for presentation at the Annual Meeting of the American Sociological Association, August 16, San Francisco, CA.

Goldstein, H. (1987), *Multilevel Models in Educational and Social Research.* London: Griffin.

Greene, W. H. (2000), *Econometric Analysis*, 4th Edition. Upper Saddle River, NJ: Prentice Hall.

Greene, W. H. (2001), "Estimating Econometric Models with Fixed Effects," Finance Department Working Paper Series, Leonard N. Stern School, New York University.

Greenland, S. (1996), "Confounding and Exposure Trends in Case-Crossover and Case-Time Control Designs," *Epidemiology*, 7, 231–239.

Hall, B. H.; Griliches, Z.; and Hausman, J. A. (1986), "Patents and R & D: Is There a Lag?" *International Economic Review*, 27 (2), 265–283.

Hatcher, L. (1994), *A Step-by-Step Approach to Using the SAS System for Factor Analysis and Structural Equation Modeling.* Cary, NC: SAS Institute Inc.

Hausman, J.; Hall, B. H.; and Griliches, Z. (1984), "Econometric Models for Count Data with an Application to the Patents-R&D Relationship," *Econometrica*, 52, 909–938.

Hu, F. B.; Goldberg, J.; Hedeker, D.; Flay, B. R.; and Pentz, M. A. (1998), "Comparison of Population-Averaged and Subject-Specific Approaches for Analyzing Repeated Binary Outcomes," *American Journal of Epidemiology*, 147, 694–703.

Johnson, N. L. and Kotz, S. (1969), *Distributions in Statistics: Discrete Distributions.* New York: John Wiley & Sons.

Judge, G.; Hill, C.; Griffiths, W.; and Lee, T. (1985), *The Theory and Practice of Econometrics.* New York: John Wiley & Sons.

Kalbfleisch, J. D. and Sprott, D. A. (1970), "Applications of Likelihood Methods to Models Involving Large Numbers of Parameters" (with discussion), *Journal of the Royal Statistical Society, Series B*, 32, 175–208.

Keane, A.; Jepson, C.; Pickett, M.; Robinson, L; and McCorkle, R. (1996), "Demographic Characteristics, Fire Experiences and Distress of Residential Fire Survivors," *Issues in Mental Health Nursing*, 17, 487–501.

Kenward, M. G. and Jones, B. (1991), "The Analysis of Categorical Data from Cross-Over Trials Using a Latent Variable Model," *Statistics in Medicine*, 10, 1607–1619.

Kline, R. B. (1998), *Principles and Practice of Structural Equation Modeling.* New York: Guilford Press, 1998.

Kreft, I. G. and De Leeuw, J. (1998), *Introducing Multilevel Modeling.* Thousand Oaks, CA: Sage Publications.

Kreft, I. G.; De Leeuw, J.; Aiken, L. (1995), "The Effects of Different Forms of Centering in Hierarchical Linear Models," *Multivariate Behavioral Research*, 30, 1–21.

LaMotte, L. R. (1983), "Fixed-, Random-, and Mixed-Effects Models," in *Encyclopedia of Statistical Sciences,* eds. S. Kotz, N. L. Johnson, and C. B. Read, New York: John Wiley & Sons.

Lin, D. Y. and Wei, L. J. (1989), "The Robust Inference for the Proportional Hazards Model," *Journal of the American Statistical Association*, 84, 1074–1078.

Maclure, M. (1991), "The Case-Crossover Design: A Method for Studying Transient Effects on the Risk of Acute Events," *American Journal of Epidemiology*, 133, 144–153.

McNemar, Q. (1955), *Psychological Statistics*. New York: John Wiley & Sons.

Mundlak, Y. (1978), "On the Pooling of Time Series and Cross Sectional Data," *Econometrica*, 56, 69–86.

Muthén, B. (1994), "Multilevel Covariance Structure Analysis," *Sociological Methods & Research*, 22, 376–398.

Muthén, B. and Curran, P. (1997), "General Longitudinal Modeling of Individual Differences in Experimental Designs: A Latent Variable Framework for Analysis and Power Estimation," *Psychological Methods*, 2, 371–402.

Neuhaus, J. M. and Kalbfleisch, J. D. (1998), "Between- and Within-Cluster Covariate Effects in the Analysis of Clustered Data," *Biometrics*, 54, 638-645.

Senn, S. (1993), *Cross-Over Trials in Clinical Research*. New York: John Wiley & Sons.

Suissa, S. (1995), "The Case-Time-Control Design," *Epidemiology*, 6, 248–253.

Teachman, J.; Duncan, G.; Yeung, J.; and Levy, D. (2001), "Covariance Structure Models for Fixed and Random Effects," *Sociological Methods & Research*, 30, 271–288.

Therneau, T. M. and Grambsch, P. (2000), *Modeling Survival Data: Extending the Cox Model*. New York: Springer-Verlag.

Tjur, T. A (1982), "Connection Between Rasch Item Analysis Model and a Multiplicative Poisson Model," *Scandinavian Journal of Statistics*, 9, 23–30.

Verbeke, G.; Spiessens, B.; and Lesaffre, E. (2001), "Conditional Linear Mixed Models," *The American Statistician*, 55, 25–34.

Waterman, R. P. and Lindsay, B. G. (1996), "Projected Score Methods for Approximating Conditional Scores," *Biometrika*, 83, 1–13.

White, H. (1980), "A Heteroscedasticity-Consistent Covariance Matrix Estimator and a Direct Test for Heteroscedasticity," *Econometrica*, 48, 817–838.

Wooldridge, J. M. (2001), *Econometric Analysis of Cross Section and Panel Data*. Cambridge, MA: MIT Press.

Index

A

ABSORB statement, GLM procedure 15, 18, 20–21
AGGREGATE option, PHREG procedure 111
AGREE option, TABLE statement (FREQ) 48
ARRAY statement, NLMIXED procedure 87
AUG option, CALIS procedure 127

B

between-subject variations 4
    fixed vs. random 5–6
bias 4
    fixed effects Cox regression 116

C

CALIS procedure 6, 125–137
    AUG option 127
    compromise between fixed effects and random effects 132–134
    COV statement 131, 133, 136
    fixed effects as latent variable model 130–132
    for fixed effects methods 130–134
    INTERCEPT option 127
    LINEQS statement 127
    random effects as latent variable model 126–130
    reciprocal effects with lagged predictors 134–137
    UCOV option 127
case-time-control design 120–123
    odds ratios 122
categorical response variables 49–78
    fixed effects vs. random effects 62–64
    hybrid method 66–70
    hybrid method, unbalanced data 38–46
    multinomial responses vs. 70–77
    multiple observations per person 57–62
    subject-specific vs. population-averaged coefficients 64–66
    two observations per person 49–57
CATMOD procedure, log-linear models 74
centering method, for fixed effects estimates 32–38
    group–mean centering 33
    unbalanced data 42–46
changeover design 3–4

CLASS statement, LOGISTIC procedure 56
CLUSTER statement, SURVEYLOGISTIC procedure 75
complete separation problem 119
compound symmetry 38
conditional logistic regression 51, 57–62, 68
conditional maximum likelihood 57–58
    Poisson models, unconditional vs. 86–92
conditional Poisson regression model 80–86
    NLMIXED procedure 87–92
    overdispersion adjustment 84–85
    time-invariant covariates 85–86
continuous response variables 9–46
    centering method 32–38
    hybrid method 32–38
    multiple observations per person 19–25
    random effects models vs. 25–32
    time-invariance of regression slopes 15–19
    two observations per person 10–15
    unbalanced data 38–46
CONTRAST statement
    GENMOD procedure 71–72
    MIXED procedure 36
CORRW option, REPEATED statement (GENMOD) 32
count data 79–105
    hybrid method 101–104
    negative binomial regression models 79, 93–97
    Poisson regression models, multiple observations per person 82–92
    Poisson regression models, two observations per person 80–86
    random effects models vs. 97–101
COV statement, CALIS procedure 131, 133, 136
COVSANDWICH (COVS) option, PHREG procedure 110–111
COVTEST option, MIXED procedure 25
Cox regression 108–112
    event history analysis with 112–116
    fixed effects with 112–116
    for conventional model 109–110
    hybrid method 116–117
    nonrepeated events 117–123
    robust variance estimation with 110–112
crossover designs 3–4
cumulative logit model 70–77

Books Available from SAS Press

Survival Analysis Using the SAS® System:
A Practical Guide
by **Paul D. Allison** .... Order No. A55233

Tuning SAS® Applications in the OS/390 and z/OS
Environments, Second Edition
by **Michael A. Raithel** .... Order No. A58172

Univariate and Multivariate General Linear Models:
Theory and Applications Using SAS® Software
by **Neil H. Timm**
and **Tammy A. Mieczkowski** .... Order No. A55809

Using SAS® in Financial Research
by **Ekkehart Boehmer, John Paul Broussard,**
and **Juha-Pekka Kallunki** .... Order No. A57601

Using the SAS® Windowing Environment: A Quick Tutorial
by **Larry Hatcher** .... Order No. A57201

Visualizing Categorical Data
by **Michael Friendly** .... Order No. A56571

Web Development with SAS® by Example
by **Frederick Pratter** .... Order No. A58694

Your Guide to Survey Research Using the SAS® System
by **Archer Gravely** .... Order No. A55688

JMP® Books

JMP® for Basic Univariate and Multivariate Statistics: A Step-by-
Step Guide
by **Ann Lehman, Norm O'Rourke, Larry Hatcher,**
and **Edward J. Stepanski** .... Order No. A59814

JMP® Start Statistics, Third Edition
by **John Sall, Ann Lehman,**
and **Lee Creighton** .... Order No. A58166

Regression Using JMP®
by **Rudolf J. Freund, Ramon C. Littell,**
and **Lee Creighton** .... Order No. A58789

support.sas.com/pubs

40 42BR 8974
FM
01/06 04-181-01 GBC